HOW TO COOK ANYTHING IN YOUR DUTCH OVEN

HOW TO COOK ANYTHING IN YOUR DUTCH OVEN

Classic American Comfort Foods and New Global Favorites

Howie Southworth and Greg Matza

Skyhorse Publishing

Skyhorse Publishing books may be purchased in bulk at special discounts for sales promotion, corporate gifts, fund-raising, or educational purposes. Special editions can also be created to specifications. For details, contact the Special Sales Department, Skyhorse Publishing, 307 West 36th Street, 11th Floor, New York, NY 10018 or info@skyhorsepublishing.com.

Visit our website at www.skyhorsepublishing.com.

10 9 8 7 6 5 4 3

Library of Congress Cataloging-in-Publication Data is available on file.

Cover design by Daniel Brount
Cover photo by Howie Southworth

Print ISBN: 978-1-5107-5114-9
Ebook ISBN: 978-1-5107-5115-6

Printed in China

Premature Corned Beef Hash, page 9

Contents

The Did You See *Big Night*?
Pasta *Timpano*, page 133

Introduction

Have you ever thought about, we mean *really* thought about the name "Dutch oven?" Truth be told, it has nothing to do with windmills or little wood shoes! *Please. Say it isn't so. We've spent our entire lives thinking that the cast-iron hero of Sunday dinner heralded from the land of tulips and bikes. Dare you challenge our dearly held culinary beliefs?*

Yes, we dare. *The Dutch oven is not Dutch*. Well, technically. But, there is some nominal relation between the classic heavy pot, stalwart of the kitchen, and Hollandic wisdom. Is *Hollandic* even a word? It should be. In the early 1700s, British metal tradesmen were casting brass cookware in lime and clay, which was laborious and expensive. A visit to the Netherlands, also engaged in molding poured metal, shined light onto the process of using sand-based molds, which were recyclable and cheaper! Thus, the "Dutch" cooking vessel was born to the British, who went on to cast easier-to-attain iron instead of brass. The Brits were rather polite to give an everlasting nod to the Dutch, no?

Cheesy Skyscraper Sandwich,
page 191

Not for nothing, but we'll mention this trivia so you have something to add to the next cocktail party, then quickly move onto the reason we wrote this book. Paul Revere, yes, the "British are coming" guy, actually invented the Dutch oven model with legs and rimmed lid you *still see* on campfire Dutch ovens. Ironic and cool, right? Okay, moving on.

The Dutch oven may well be the perfect cooking vessel, but for shallow frying, and except perhaps for baking. But, what if we told you that the Dutch oven can surprise you? That heavy bottom? Those tall sides? The lid? Ideal for everything from braising and stewing to simmering and casseroles. Soups and roasts cry out for the even, universal heat. Most warming, comforting dishes reserve the Dutch oven as a savior and we will show you how it's done.

Our title, *How to Cook Anything in Your Dutch Oven*, may be a tad hyperbolic, but we strive to provide you with a diverse set of recipes perfect for that necessarily bulky kitchen character. In these pages exist everything from chicken soup and gumbo to mac and cheese and brownies. The dish names may be fun and the concepts familiar, but the techniques and results are the real hallmarks of this ode to cast-iron perfection. To boot, the flavor combinations and unique applications will also make you the star of any upcoming neighborhood potluck.

You know, the more we think about the word *Dutch*, the more confused we get. "Going Dutch?" You know, when everyone pays their own way at a dinner or a night out at the local bar? How about "Double Dutch," where two long jump ropes encircle a player at high speed in opposite directions? "Dutch Baby" pancakes with those super-puffy edges? Deep, dark "Dutch Process" cocoa powder? None of the above have anything to do with canals or pot cafés . . . wait, except maybe that last one. Is anyone else getting the munchies? Mmmm, brownies (see page 225).

Chapter 1
BRAISES

Vampire-Proof Meatballs

You put *how much* garlic in here?

When you look at this recipe, you might think to yourself, *wow, that's a lot of garlic*. And you'd be right. But, if I just fed this dish to you, you'd probably never guess that there's much garlic at all and wonder about the secret ingredient. Why? You simply won't believe what braising garlic in a bath of lemon juice will do to it. It becomes soft, mild, and rich. After 15 to 20 minutes, the cloves begin to dissolve, adding body to the sauce. I've served this dish dozens of times, and I've rarely had anyone refuse seconds. Give it a try and find out for yourself!

—Greg

TOTAL TIME: 1 hour, 10 minutes | **VESSEL:** 4½+ qt Dutch oven | **SERVES:** 4–6

FOR THE MEATBALLS:

1 lb ground beef
½ cup bread crumbs
1 small onion, grated or diced finely
1 large egg
4 Tbsp parsley, chopped
½ tsp ground black pepper
1 tsp salt

FOR THE SAUCE:

2 Tbsp extra-virgin olive oil
Juice of 6 lemons
½ cup water
1 tsp salt
2 heads garlic, about 20–25 cloves, peeled
1 cup bottled artichoke hearts, drained

Preheat the oven to 350°F.

In a large mixing bowl, thoroughly combine beef, bread crumbs, onion, egg, parsley, pepper, and salt. Form into 20 to 25 small meatballs.

Grease the bottom of a Dutch oven with the olive oil and place the meatballs into the pot. Place the pot, uncovered, into the oven and roast the meatballs for 20 minutes, or until well browned. If the meatballs don't all fit in the bottom of the pot, don't panic! Just throw the extras in another skillet, roasting pan, or baking sheet.

Remove the meatballs from the pot, leaving the juices. Deglaze the pot with lemon juice, water, and 1 teaspoon of salt, using a wooden spoon to scrape all the brown bits from the bottom of the pot. Add garlic, and place back in the oven, covered, for 25 to 30 minutes, or until the garlic is tender.

Add the meatballs and artichoke hearts into the pot, and place it, covered, back in the oven for a final 15 minutes.

Remove the pot from the oven. Best served over rice, accompanied by broccoli, asparagus, or another vegetable that loves lemon.

Doro What? *Doro WAT!*

Spicy Ethiopian braised chicken

If you've never tried Ethiopian food, you need to. It's the stuff of which memories are made, if only for the uniqueness of the experience. A bright array of tiny food mountains atop injera, or what appears to be an extremely large, soft and thin, crumpet. Ripping off a piece of injera and pinching at the colorful mounds, each bite is a communal gastronomic event. I will also go out on a limb and say that you *do* or *will* remember your first time. Who are my go-to stars of the feast? *Kitfo*, a version of beef tartare, *mesir wat*, luxurious split red lentils, *gomen*, braised collard greens, and the queen, the national dish of Ethiopia, *doro wat*, spiced chicken in an unlikely sauce made almost *entirely out of onions*.

—Howie

TOTAL TIME: 2 hours | **VESSEL:** 5–6 qt Dutch oven | **SERVES:** 4–6

- 3 lb chicken pieces, bone-in, skin removed
- Juice of 1 lemon
- 1 Tbsp, plus 2 tsp kosher salt, divided
- ¼ cup extra-virgin olive oil
- 3 large red onions, pulsed in food processor until very fine
- ½ cup berbere or hot chile powder
- ½ cup *nit'r kibe* spiced butter or unsalted butter
- 2 Tbsp tomato paste
- 4 cloves garlic, minced
- 1 Tbsp ginger, minced
- 2 cups dry red wine
- 2 cups chicken stock or water
- 6 hard-boiled eggs, peeled (optional)

Preheat the oven to 325°F.

In a large mixing bowl, rub the chicken pieces with lemon juice and 1 tablespoon of salt. Set aside.

Add olive oil to a Dutch oven over medium-low heat. When the oil begins to shimmer, add the onions and salt and cook, covered, stirring occasionally until the onions are very soft, about 30 to 40 minutes. Stir in berbere or chile powder, *nit'r kibe* or butter, tomato paste, garlic, and ginger, cover, and continue to cook, stirring occasionally, until the mixture has darkened to a deep reddish brown and has the texture of an onion jam, about an additional 15 to 20 minutes.

Stir in wine and stock or water, increase the heat to medium-high and bring to a boil. Reduce the heat to low and submerge the seasoned chicken pieces. Transfer the pot to the oven and braise for 1 hour. If using hard-boiled eggs, after 45 minutes, submerge the peeled eggs in the liquid and continue to braise for 15 minutes.

Remove the *doro wat* from the oven. Serve pieces of chicken with plenty of onion sauce. Traditionally, it is served with fresh injera (Ethiopian pancake) or rice, maybe a squeeze of additional lemon.

Oh, Kale Yeah!

Finally, a version that tastes great

Admit it. If scientists declared that potatoes just beat out kale as the latest, greatest superfood, we would all scream a collective *Woohoo!* Cue the massive crowds racing toward the nearest baked potato bar.

But, alas, kale is still a superfood. And the taste of it is likely to cue those same crowds to give up and race to the nearest donut shop. Innumerable attempts have been made to slip it into unsuspecting host foods. Kale chocolate cake. Great. Green smoothies. Check. Antioxidant lasagna. *Stop. It. Now!* Truth be told, I get it. I do. It's fabulously *good* for you, like therapy or, um, taxes.

What if there was a magical formula that would allow the improbable deliciousness of kale to spring from its dark and crinkly leaves? Friends, there is a way. This fantastic cocktail of punchy garlic, sweet caramelized onions, and soy sauce somehow transports kale from "thing to be snuck into brownies" to "Hey, that's pretty good. Can I have some more?"

—Greg

TOTAL TIME: 1 hour, 20 minutes | **VESSEL:** 4–5 qt Dutch oven | **SERVES:** 8–10

- 3 Tbsp extra-virgin olive oil
- 1 large onion, sliced into ¼-inch strips
- 1 tsp kosher salt
- 6 cloves garlic, roughly chopped
- 6 cups chicken or vegetable stock
- ¼ cup soy sauce
- 20 oz kale, ribs and leaves roughly chopped

Add oil to a Dutch oven over medium-low heat. When the oil begins to shimmer, add the onion and salt and sauté for 15 to 20 minutes or until the onion is very soft and has begun to caramelize. Add the garlic and continue to sauté for 1 to 2 minutes, or until very fragrant. Add the stock and soy sauce, increase the heat to medium-high, and bring to a boil.

Reduce the heat to low and maintain a simmer. Add the kale in batches until wilted. Cover the pot and allow the kale to simmer for 1 hour. Serve as a surprisingly healthy and even more surprisingly delicious side dish.

Premature Corned Beef Hash

Okay, it's corned beef and cabbage

From the moment my Dad unleashed a gelatinous loaf of what appeared to be some sort of meat and potato goop, and with a deft hand armed with a spatula, flattened it out on a scorchingly hot pan, I fell in love with canned corned beef hash. Enamored by the thin, crispy exterior, the steamy, creamy center, and that salty, earthy bite of cured meat, I was in. As it turned out, I was in deep. That delicious on-ramp to chemically tenderized meat sent me on a lifelong search for the best expressions of corned beef, its ancient ancestors, and its global descendants.

My quest to find perfectly auburn, meltingly tender corned beef has led me to the deserts of Northwest China, the tundras of Russia, the smokehouses of Istanbul, and naturally, the land of *Darby O'Gill and the Little People*. What I found in Ireland may seem surprising. Yes, the Irish have been masters of curing beef for hundreds of years. But, perhaps ironically, most Irish considered beef to be a luxury item, as bovines were more valued for their field work than their role at the dinner table. Thus, exporting most of the beef that was cured made good sense. This leads us back to the US of A.

Where *bacon and cabbage* was a classic and celebrated Irish meal, corned beef was easier to buy for new Irish immigrants in the early 20th century. So, yes, *corned beef and cabbage* for St. Patty's Day is indeed an (Irish-) American innovation. Of course, it's also become a quite popular way to mark St. Pat's for millions of American homes (coming in a close second to green beer). Nonetheless, I make a damned fine corned beef and cabbage and here it is in all its glory. But, can you keep a secret? My ultimate goal is to harvest the leftovers the next morning, chop them up good, and introduce them to a scorchingly hot pan. Ah. My beloved corned beef hash.

—Howie

TOTAL TIME: 5 hours, 40 minutes | **VESSEL:** 6–7 qt Dutch oven | **SERVES:** 8–10

- 1 large yellow onion, sliced into ¼-inch strips
- 3 lb corned beef brisket
- 10 cups water, more as needed
- 12 oz dark beer
- 10 cloves garlic, lightly crushed
- 2 tsp black peppercorns
- 1½ lb red potatoes
- 1 head red or green cabbage, cored, sliced into ¼-inch strips
- 1 lb baby carrots
- 3 Tbsp extra-virgin olive oil
- ½ bunch parsley, roughly chopped

Preheat the oven to 275°F.

In a Dutch oven over high heat, place onion and corned beef, add water, beer, garlic, and peppercorns and bring the liquid to a boil. Place the lid on the pot and transfer to the oven to braise for 5 hours.

(Directions continued on next page)

Carefully remove the pot from the oven and uncover. Carefully transfer the corned beef to a cutting board, cover with aluminum foil, and let it rest while you prepare the vegetables. Place the pot over medium-high heat. Add potatoes and simmer for 10 minutes. Add cabbage and carrots and simmer for an additional 20 minutes.

Transfer the potatoes to a platter. Using a potato masher or a large fork, slightly smash the potatoes, drizzle with olive oil, and garnish with parsley. Transfer the cabbage and carrots to a separate platter. Carve the corned beef across the grain, top with remaining parsley, and serve with accompanying vegetables.

Thanksgiving Never Looked So Bashful

Chinese red-cooked turkey

When I moved to China in 1996, aside from being unexpectedly deified for my mountain-man-like beard, I was taken aback by the myriad cooking techniques that seldom leave Chinese shores. Wonderful stuff that, if adopted abroad, could turn styles like American Chinese food, or really any genre of food, on their collective ear. *Red-cooking* is one of these memorable methods. It's essentially a long-braising technique generally used to make tougher cuts of meats fall-apart tender with a tad sweet, slightly salty, subtly aromatic tone. Strangely, any meat undergoing this flavor bombardment ends up tasting beefier, porkier, chickenier than by any other cooking method. But, what about turkey?

Aside from the occasional deli sandwich or a healthier burger after seeing one's cardiologist, do we truly consider the turkey but once a year on Thanksgiving? Even then, it's pretty typical to see family plates loaded up with sundry side dishes and a wisp or two of roasted bird drowning in gravy. Mmm, delicious gravy. Being honest, turkey gets the shaft and should be celebrated more. After trying this traditional Chinese treatment of turkey, you'll be hooked. Oh, and tell your cardiologist I said, "you're welcome."

—Howie

TOTAL TIME: 3 hours | **VESSEL:** 5–6 qt Dutch oven | **SERVES:** 4–6

- 2 lb turkey breast, bone-in, skin-on
- 1 tsp kosher salt
- 3 Tbsp canola or vegetable oil
- 8 scallions, whole
- ½ bunch cilantro, stems separated, leaves roughly chopped
- 8 cloves garlic, lightly crushed
- 2 inches ginger, crushed
- 1 cup Shaoxing or other Chinese rice wine, or dry sherry
- 5 cups water
- 3 Tbsp soy sauce
- 3 Tbsp mushroom or other dark soy sauce
- 2 Tbsp Chinese black vinegar or balsamic vinegar
- 2 Tbsp dark brown sugar
- 2 tsp Chinese five-spice powder

Preheat the oven to 325°F. Rub the turkey with salt.

Heat the oil in a Dutch oven over medium-high heat. When the oil begins to shimmer, place the turkey skin-side down in the pot. After 3 to 4 minutes as the skin has browned, flip the turkey and continue to brown for 2 to 3 minutes.

Using a slotted spoon or tongs, remove the turkey from the pot and set aside. Cover the bottom of the pot with scallions, cilantro stems, garlic, and ginger. Place the browned

(Directions continued on page 13)

turkey atop the vegetables, skin-side down. In a mixing bowl, thoroughly whisk together the remaining ingredients, and pour into the pot, being sure not to disrupt the vegetables and meat.

Bring the pot to a visible simmer. Turn off the heat, cover the pot with a lid, transfer to the oven and braise for 2 hours. Remove the pot from the oven.

Let the uncovered pot rest on the stove for 15 minutes before skimming fat from the surface of the liquid and removing the turkey. Garnish with chopped cilantro leaves and serve with the rest of a Thanksgiving feast, or more humbly, with rice and a bit of the sauce from the pot.

Passover Ain't Over 'Til this Brisket Sings

A traditional roast, the Matza way

Calling this a recipe is a bit embarrassing. But, I've had a lot of bad brisket, and enough is enough. Bad brisket is extremely painful because it is dead simple to make it brilliant. There are two keys to making this one successful—the right wine and the right slice.

The wine: Don't get fancy. Go cheap. Go sweet. Go Concord Grape. After all, you're looking to the wine to offer up its acidity and alcohol to help tenderize the meat. You're not looking for a fine bouquet, earthy tones, or the right terroir. The brisket cooks way too long for any of that to survive.

The slice: Carve the meat when it is still tough. This way, the slices won't shred apart when braising. It's also a great workout for arm day.

—Greg

TOTAL TIME: 3 hours + overnight | **VESSEL:** 6 qt or larger Dutch oven | **SERVES:** 10–12

- 4 lb brisket—aim for one shaped more like a triangle
- 1 large onion, sliced into ¼-inch strips
- 1 package onion soup mix
- ½ bottle Manischevitz or other sweet wine

Preheat the oven to 350°F.

Place the brisket in a Dutch oven. Layer the onion strips over the meat. Sprinkle with the onion soup and pour in the wine. Cover tightly and braise it in the oven for 70 minutes.

Remove the brisket to a cutting board, keeping the onion strips and gravy in the Dutch oven. Allow the brisket to rest and cool for at least 15 minutes. Once it has cooled a bit, slice across the grain of the meat, cutting the brisket into just under ½-inch slices. The meat will be tough at this point—don't worry about it. Add the sliced meat back into the Dutch oven. Cover and refrigerate overnight.

The next day, place the pot back in a 350°F oven and allow it to warm and simmer for 60 minutes. Remove from the oven and serve with matzo ball soup, gefilte fish, and horseradish.

Bathe Your Butt in Beer

Tipsy and succulent braised pork shoulder

Frankly, it was much more fun to write that title than it was to use "Bathe Your Shoulder in Beer!" But, have you ever wondered why pork shoulder is alternatively referred to as "Boston Butt?" No, it has nothing to do with the rear of the pig, that's where ham comes from. Nor is it some criticism of Bostonians and their tendency to get porcine anatomy backward. Not actually a thing, but wouldn't *that* be awesome? Perhaps more boringly, New England butchers of the 1700s would store cheaper cuts of meat in barrels, or in old English, "buttis." Sheesh, can't catch a comedic break here.

One has to wonder, however, if the ham, the belly, *and* the shoulder of pork were all stored in these "buttis," how did the shoulder get stuck with the pricelessly entertaining word "butt" where "ham" and "belly" get to keep their relatively straight-laced names? We may never know. But, we do know that beer and pork are extremely well paired.

—Greg

TOTAL TIME: 4 hours, 30 minutes | **VESSEL:** 5–6 qt Dutch oven | **SERVES:** 4–6

- 2½ lb boneless Boston butt pork or pork shoulder, cut into 2-inch cubes
- 1 tsp kosher salt
- 3 Tbsp canola or vegetable oil
- 4 leeks, whiter parts trimmed, halved longwise and washed
- 10 cloves garlic, lightly crushed
- 2 cups stout or other dark beer
- 3 cups water
- 4 tablespoons soy sauce
- 3 tablespoons red wine vinegar
- 2 tablespoons mushroom or other dark soy sauce
- 3 Tbsp dark brown sugar
- 1 Tbsp ground cumin

Preheat the oven to 275°F. Rub the pork belly with salt.

Heat the oil in a Dutch oven over medium-high heat. When the oil begins to shimmer, start to brown the pork pieces in batches so as to not overcrowd the pot. Be sure to brown each side, about 4 to 6 minutes in total.

Using a slotted spoon, remove the pork from the pot and set aside. Cover the bottom of the pot with leek halves and garlic cloves. Place the pork atop the vegetables. In a mixing bowl, whisk together the remaining ingredients, and pour into the pot, making your best effort not to disrupt the layers of vegetables and pork.

Increase the heat up to high and bring the pot to a boil. Reduce the heat to medium-high and allow the mixture to high-simmer for 10 minutes. Cover the pot with a lid, transfer to the oven, and braise for 3½ hours. Carefully remove the lid and use a fork to check if the pork is beginning to fall apart. If it is not yet, return the covered pot to the oven and braise for an additional 30 minutes. If it is, remove the pot from the oven.

Let the uncovered pot rest on the stove for 15 minutes before skimming fat from the surface of the liquid and removing the pork pieces intact, as best you can. Serve on a sandwich or with rice and a bit of the sauce from the pot.

Yes, Grandma, We'll Call It Gravy

Sunday just wouldn't be the same without it

When I was a kid, we frequently drove up to Union City, New Jersey, from down the shore to see my grandparents, cousins, uncles, aunts, and of course, the "aunts, uncles, and cousins." The extended Italian American family can get confusing with a family tree that has as many imaginary and dotted branches as it does solid. Although as we drove up the parkway and my young brain was trying to predict just who it was that we were about to see, whether related or related-ish, my mental focus was always drawn back to the meal that was already being prepared.

Most Sundays, I could count on the arrival scene being the same. Sausages and neck bones being browned in the tall pot. The meatballs just about done being fried in a separate pan. Paper-towel-lined countertops—never figured that one out. My grandmother would sneak me a preview meatball in a tiny bowl, *shhh*! All the meats would then take a nice long bath in simmering tomato puree and maybe some other stuff. To ask about Grandma's recipe or to call this *tomato sauce* got a kid chased from kitchen with a hot spoon! It's *gravy*, and yes, *there is a difference*!

The Italians have different words for *sauce* and *gravy*, so why shouldn't we pay attention? *Salsa* is a coating/topping made from fruits, vegetables, or cheese, and is the literal translation of sauce. *Sugo*, on the other hand, is often mistranslated as *sauce* as well, but is a coating/topping that includes meats or bones. Boom. Got it?

—Howie

TOTAL TIME: 4 hours, 30 minutes | Equipment: 7+ qt Dutch oven | **SERVES:** 8–10

FOR THE MEATBALLS (14–16):

1 lb stale bread, torn into pieces
2 lb ground beef
3 cloves garlic, minced
2 eggs
1 tsp salt
¼ cup Parmesan cheese, grated or shredded
½ tsp ground black pepper
½ cup roughly chopped parsley

FOR THE GRAVY:

3 Tbsp extra-virgin olive oil
1 lb pork neck bones or spare ribs
2 lb Italian sausage links
4 cloves garlic, roughly chopped
3 Tbsp tomato paste
2 cups red wine
3 (28-oz) cans tomatoes, pureed
1 qt All The Bones Broth (page 93) or chicken stock
2 Tbsp dried oregano
1 tsp sugar
2 tsp salt
1 tsp ground black pepper

(Directions on next page)

TO MAKE THE MEATBALLS:

Preheat the oven to 400°F and prepare a lightly greased sheet pan. In a colander, lightly spray and toss the stale bread with water until just soaked through. Using clean hands, mush the bread so it turns into a paste and drains of excess water. Remove bread paste to a large mixing bowl and add the remaining ingredients. Evenly combine the ingredients with your hands. Form the meat mixture into golf-sized balls and place on the sheet pan. Roast in the oven for 30 minutes, remove from the oven, cover with foil, and set aside. Reduce the oven temperature to 275°F.

TO START THE GRAVY:

Heat the oil in a Dutch oven over medium-high heat. When the oil begins to shimmer, working in batches so as not to overcrowd the pot, sauté the neck bones or ribs and sausages until they brown on all sides, about 4 to 6 minutes per batch, removing meat to a plate as they are browned. Add garlic and tomato paste to the hot oil and sauté for 1 minute. Add the red wine into the pot and allow the wine to reduce by half, about 6 to 8 minutes. Add the tomato puree, broth or stock, oregano, sugar, salt, and pepper.

Bring the mixture to a simmer, turn off the heat, add the browned neck bones or ribs and sausage and transfer the uncovered pot to the oven to braise for 3 hours. Carefully remove the pot from the oven, submerge the reserved meatballs into the gravy, place a lid on the pot, and let it rest for at least 45 minutes.

Remove the meat from the gravy and serve on a separate platter. Serve atop the Polenta Without the Workout from page 187, use as a sauce for Seriously Tall Eggplant Parm from page 159, mix into cooked pasta, and/or serve alongside fresh bread.

Osso Buco

'Cause it's fun to say

Osso buco is an object lesson in economics. I got a charitable B-minus in Econ 101, so I'm not sure exactly what that lesson is, but there's definitely something there.

You see, for centuries, this was a peasant dish. The rich ate high off the veal—the tenderloin, the sirloin, the sweetbreads. And the poor were left with the gristly legs that were more bone than flesh. But then, somewhere in the past 50 years, the magic happened. The cheap, almost throwaway leg meat, was transformed into a delicacy. Was it marketing? Was it branding? Was it supply and demand? I have no idea. Again—B-minus in Econ here. But something happened, such that a pound of veal leg became among the most expensive cuts of the animal.

While I can't tell you why the veal leg is so expensive, I can tell you why it is so delicious. All those connective tissues that make the meat so incredibly tough—when exposed to low heat for a long time, they turn into a silky gelatin whose taste and texture puts those tenderloins to shame. So, splurge a little—make some osso buco. And try not to focus on why it costs so darn much.

—Greg

TOTAL TIME: 2 hours, 30 minutes | **VESSEL:** 5–6 qt Dutch oven | **SERVES:** 4–6

FOR THE MEAT:

6 veal shanks
½ cup all-purpose flour
2 tsp salt, divided
½ tsp ground black pepper
1 Tbsp extra-virgin olive oil
2 onions, diced
2 carrots, diced
2 ribs celery, diced
2 Tbsp tomato paste
2 cups white wine
1 cup water
½ tsp dried thyme
2 bay leaves

FOR THE GREMOLATA TOPPING:

6 cloves garlic, minced or pressed
2 Tbsp lemon zest, grated
½ cup parsley, chopped

Preheat the oven to 325°F.

Using butcher's twine, tie a loop around the circumference of each shank, so that the bone doesn't fall away as it cooks. Don't worry about what kind of knot—no Scout leader will be judging you. Just tie it tightly.

Season the flour by adding 1 teaspoon salt and ½ teaspoon pepper. Place the seasoned flour on a plate, and lightly dredge each veal shank, shaking off excess flour.

Add olive oil to a Dutch oven over medium-high heat. When the oil begins to shimmer, add 3 of the shanks. Fry for 5 minutes or until lightly browned, and flip. Fry another 5 minutes and remove. Repeat with the other 3 shanks, and set the meat aside.

Add the onions, carrots, and celery to the pot. Scrape the bottom of the pan to pull up any delicious brown

(Directions continued on page 23)

bits, and sauté for 6 to 8 minutes, or until the onions are lightly browned. Add the tomato paste and mix it around to coat the vegetables. Continue to sauté for another 2 minutes, or until the tomato just starts to darken.

Pour in the wine and water and scrape the bottom of the pan to pull up any new brown bits. Add the thyme and bay leaves, the remaining teaspoon of salt, and the browned veal shanks. Cover and place in the oven for 90 minutes.

While the shanks are bubbling, create the gremolata by combining the garlic, lemon zest, and parsley.

Remove the pot from the oven. Using tongs, gently pull out the shanks, reserving them on a plate. Place the Dutch oven over medium-low heat and allow the gravy to reduce for about 5 minutes. While it is reducing, snip the twine around each shank.

Remove the bay leaves, and serve by pouring gravy over the shanks, then topping with gremolata.

Carnitas Are Super Easy

Don't tell your local taco joint

Slow-cooked pork has been applied to hundreds, nay, thousands of recipes across the world since Porky was domesticated, some 9,000 years ago. From China's favorite red-cooked pork to that French countryside darling, cassoulet. From Brazil's national dish of feijoada to down-home North Carolina BBQ.

I've gotten down deep with many of the global takes on fatty pork, specifically shoulder, and let me tell you, it's one of the easiest meat preparations you will ever encounter. Since it cooks for so long, many recipes even skip time-consuming sautéing and searing and throw everything in a pot. Look, you can keep this between us and wow your dinner guests with not only the delectably complicated aroma of your home, but a final platter of shredded, meaty gold that gives the impression of a project. This take on carnitas is both classic and updated to give a hint of BBQ and the exotic East . . . with very little effort. You're welcome.

—Howie

TOTAL TIME: 4 hours, 30 minutes | **VESSEL:** 3–5 qt Dutch oven | **SERVES:** 4–6

- 1 onion, quartered
- 10 cloves garlic, crushed
- 1½ Tbsp kosher salt
- 1 Tbsp ground cumin
- 1 Tbsp smoked paprika
- Juice of 1 lime
- 3 Tbsp dark soy sauce
- 2½–3 lb pork shoulder, boneless, cut into 2-inch pieces
- Water to cover

Preheat the oven to 325°F.

In a Dutch oven, combine all ingredients and bring to a simmer over medium-high heat. Cover with a lid and transfer to the oven to braise for 3 to 3½ hours, or until the pork easily pulls apart with a fork. Remove the pot from the oven and let it rest, covered, for 1 hour.

Using a slotted spoon, transfer the pork pieces from the broth to a cutting board. Using two forks, shred the pork. One option for serving is to spread the pork on a sheet pan and return to a 375°F. oven to get some crispy bits. Another option is to mix shreds of pork with a bit of the broth from the pot. Serve as a taco filling, or as a main with rice and Those Beans from That Mexican Place on page 52.

Cooler than Cola

Root beer–braised short ribs

Cooking meats in cola is a tried and true method of building a sweet and savory dish without buying dozens of exotic pantry ingredients that you may never use again. But, since cola can be bought nearly anywhere on the planet, global cooks have caught on to this trend. From Korean kalbi marinade and Chinese braised wings to Filipino adobo pork and Cuban shredded beef, cola-infused cooking is a world phenomenon well outside the American box. This recipe rips a page out of many different culinary traditions and somehow works. What's better? Bringing the dish directly back to the American kitchen and using *root beer* instead of cola. That funky and weird soda you just can't find anywhere else. Americana at its finest, and truly unique.

—Greg

TOTAL TIME: 3 hours, 30 minutes | **VESSEL:** 4–6 qt Dutch oven | **SERVES:** 4–6

3 lb beef short ribs, bone-in
1 tsp kosher salt
½ tsp ground black pepper
3 Tbsp extra-virgin olive oil
1 large onion, sliced into ¼-inch strips
4 cloves garlic, roughly chopped
3 Tbsp flour
2½ cups beef or chicken stock
2½ cups root beer
⅓ cup soy sauce, ideally dark
2 Tbsp dried oregano

Preheat the oven to 325°F. In a large mixing bowl, rub the short ribs with salt and pepper.

Heat the oil in a Dutch oven over medium-high heat. When the oil begins to shimmer, start to brown the short ribs in batches so as to not overcrowd the pot. Be sure to brown at least the wide sides, about 4 to 6 minutes per batch. Set the short ribs aside.

Add the onion to the pot and sauté for 6 to 8 minutes, or until soft and beginning to brown. Add the garlic and continue to sauté for 1 minute. Sprinkle the flour into the pot and stir into the onion and garlic until no white flour is visible.

Pour in the stock, root beer, and soy sauce. Bring the mixture to a boil, then turn off the heat. Stir in the oregano and submerge the short ribs. Place the lid on the pot and transfer to the oven to braise for 2½ to 3 hours, or until the meat is falling from the bone.

Remove the pot from the oven and serve the short ribs along with some of the sauce atop rice, or with a potato creation.

Adobo Entendre

An ironic Filipino braised pork belly

The word "adobo" in modern culinary circles means a great number of things. The term was originally used in Spain to mean a marinade or paste that helped preserve foods. It was largely built on acids, salts, and spices meant to cure meats that would otherwise go to waste. Adobo has always had the lovely side effect of adding robust flavors to meats.

As the Spanish and Portuguese went about conquering the world, the name "adobo" was appointed to a wider range of culinary treatments. Notably in Mexico, adobo morphed into a preservation method for chiles, which lead to the ever-popular chipotles in adobo.

In the Philippines, the departure from the Spanish tradition is even more extreme. Adobo is not a marinade and adobo is not a sauce. Adobo became a method of braising meats in vinegar. Yeah, I'm that guy who avoided Easter egg festivities since the smell of vinegar repulsed me so. Imagine me, decades later, falling in love with a recipe for Filipino adobo pork belly that actually draws me closer!

—Howie

TOTAL TIME: 3 hours | **VESSEL:** 4–5 qt Dutch oven | **SERVES:** 4–6

2 Tbsp canola or vegetable oil
2 lb pork belly, skin on, cut into 2-inch pieces
5 cloves garlic, roughly chopped
2 leeks, trimmed, halved, washed
2 cups water
½ cup soy sauce, preferably dark
½ cup white vinegar
½ tsp salt
1 Tbsp honey
2 tsp black peppercorns
3 scallions, thinly sliced

Preheat the oven to 325°F.

Heat the oil in a Dutch oven over medium-high heat. When the oil begins to shimmer, start to brown the pork pieces in batches so as to not overcrowd the pot. Be sure to brown each side, about 4 to 6 minutes in total. Add garlic and sauté until fragrant, 30 to 45 seconds. Add the remaining ingredients and stir to ensure the honey has melted. Bring the mixture to a boil and remove from the heat.

Cover the pot and transfer to the oven and braise for 2 hours. Carefully uncover the pot and continue to braise for an additional 30 minutes. Remove the pot from the oven and transfer the pork belly to a serving platter and carve slices, garnish with scallions. Carefully pour the sauce through a strainer into a separate bowl. Serve the meat and sauce separately with white rice.

Islander Sweet-and-Sour Beef Ribs

Meat that makes you wanna hula

If you are interested in authentic Hawaiian fare, avoid this dish. This is more like what people in Columbus, Ohio, understood that people in Hawaii were eating, based on what they saw in that *Brady Bunch* special. If the recipe were authentic, television logic also says that evil tikis cause surfing wipeouts, tarantulas creep around Honolulu hotels, and hula causes backs to go out. Though, that last one may be true.

Back to meat. Those people of Columbus, Ohio, may have really been onto something. Most short-rib dishes lean into the meatiness of the cut—adding butter, wine, mushrooms, and other deep, rich flavors. This recipe goes the opposite direction, cutting through that richness with the brightness of vinegar, tomatoes, pineapple, and sugar.

So, strap on that coconut bra, slap on some Coppertone, and let's eat some Islander Sweet-and-Sour Beef Ribs! Do avoid hula, though. If it could take down Alice, it can take down anyone.

—Greg

TOTAL TIME: 3 hours | **VESSEL:** 6 qt Dutch oven | **SERVES:** 4–6

- 4 lb. beef short ribs, about 12 ribs
- 2 tsp salt
- 1 tsp oil
- 1 cup ketchup
- 1 cup vinegar
- ½ cup water
- 5 Tbsp brown sugar
- ½ tsp hot mustard powder
- 2 Tbsp molasses
- 1 onion, diced
- 1 green pepper, diced
- 20 oz can pineapple chunks, packed in juice

Preheat the oven to 225°F.

Rub the ribs with salt. Add oil to a Dutch oven over medium heat. When the oil begins to shimmer, add as many ribs as comfortably fit in the pan. You will likely need to do this in two batches. Brown the ribs on all sides except the bone side, about 6 to 10 minutes for each batch until all meat has been browned.

Place the browned ribs into the pot, cover with a lid, and transfer to the oven to roast for 90 to 120 minutes, the longer the better. Remove the ribs from the oven and uncover.

In a mixing bowl, combine the ketchup, vinegar, water, brown sugar, mustard, and molasses. Stir until combined. Add the onion, green pepper, and pineapple, along with the sauce mixture into the Dutch oven with the ribs.

Over medium heat, bring the mixture to a light simmer. Turn the heat to low, cover, and allow to cook for 30 minutes. Remove from the heat and uncover. Before serving, taste the sauce, and add a touch of salt and/or vinegar to brighten it up. Serve with white or brown rice and a crisp green salad.

When 2-Cup Chicken Just Isn't Enough

Chinese 3-cup chicken

Chinese cuisine is often seen as complicated, with too many hard-to-find ingredients and methods that bridge the worlds of acrobatics and cooking. Huge fires leaping from scalding woks, expertly pleated dumplings, noodle dough being pulled, twisted, and stretched thinner than thin. It's amazing. However, equally amazing are the preparations from the Chinese countryside—beyond simple and outrageously delicious.

One of my favorites is 3-cup chicken. Traditionally, the recipe is 1 cup sesame oil, 1 cup rice wine, and 1 cup soy sauce. I messed with it a bit, cutting back on the oil and throwing in some extras. But the core is the same—toss a few things in a pot, take a nap, and awake hours later to a gastronomic miracle. This succulent, deep, rich chicken will convince your guests that you've spent months in training with Chinese masters.

—Greg

TOTAL TIME: 1 hour | **VESSEL:** 4–5 qt Dutch oven | **SERVES:** 4–6

½ cup roasted sesame oil
10 cloves garlic, smashed
1 inch ginger, smashed
6 scallions, white and green parts separated, thinly sliced
3 green or red jalapeño peppers, thinly sliced
2 lb chicken thighs, boneless, skinless
1 cup Shaoxing, other Chinese rice wine or dry sherry
1 cup soy sauce
1 Tbsp granulated sugar

Preheat the oven to 300°F.

Heat oil in a Dutch oven over medium-high heat. When the oil begins to shimmer, add garlic, ginger, scallion whites, and peppers and sauté until fragrant, 2 to 3 minutes. Add chicken, rice wine or sherry, soy sauce, and sugar, and bring to a boil, then remove from the heat. Cover the pot and transfer to the oven to braise for 50 minutes.

Remove the pot from the oven, uncover, garnish with scallion greens, and serve with rice.

Man Bites Shark

Mmm, creamy spicy shark

I am on the fence as to whether or not to watch *Jaws* with my kids. We just got back from a few brilliant days on Martha's Vineyard. So, on one hand, it would make perfect sense to screen this most amazing feat of storytelling on the heels of riding our bikes through all of the actual scenery from the film. On the other hand, one of my great pleasure in life is to play in the ocean with my boys. Which, if they do see it, may never happen again.

The funny thing about *Jaws* is that I watched it as a kid myself, and loved the feeling of cinematic anxiety and terror. Despite the movie's message that one never knows what lurks beneath, I happily skipped back to the waves. But then I grew up and watched it again. Woah. Completely different experience. Perhaps it was the relatively new feeling of mortality. Maybe it was my ready access to the news and hearing of shark attacks across the globe. I admit that though I think about *Jaws* about half the time I step away from shore, it doesn't prevent my fun. What it does do, however, is inspire ways in which I plan to introduce the beasts to my kitchen. *Hey boys! Make some popcorn!*

—Howie

TOTAL TIME: 1 hour | **VESSEL:** 3+ qt Dutch oven | **SERVES:** 3–4

- 1½–2 lb shark, mahi-mahi, or swordfish fillets or steaks
- Juice of 1 lime
- 2 tsp kosher salt, divided
- 5 Tbsp extra-virgin olive oil
- 1 large onion, sliced into ¼-inch strips
- 4 cloves garlic, roughly chopped
- 2 (13.5-oz) cans coconut milk
- 3 Tbsp dry sherry
- 1 tsp ground black pepper
- 1 tsp smoked paprika
- 1–2 tbsp chile paste (optional)
- Cilantro leaves for garnish

Preheat the oven to 275°F. Marinate shark or other fish fillets with lime juice and 1 teaspoon of salt and set aside.

Add oil to a Dutch oven over medium heat. When the oil begins to shimmer, add onion and sauté until very soft and beginning to brown, about 15 to 20 minutes. Add garlic and remaining 1 teaspoon of salt and continue to sauté for 2 minutes. Pour in coconut milk and sherry and bring to a light boil. Stir in black pepper, paprika, and chile paste, if using. Reduce the heat to low and simmer until slightly thickened, about 20 minutes.

Turn off the heat and add salted fish to the liquid. Transfer the pot to the oven and braise until the fish is easily pierced with a fork, about 10 to 15 minutes. Remove the pot from the oven, garnish with cilantro, and serve. Goes great with steamy white rice and a screening of *Jaws*.

Pot Roast

Yep—pot roast

Pity the poor pot roast. Perpetually persecuted. Pulled from potlucks at precisely the point where people pondered the performance of this provision on their pulmonary health. People preferred poultry! People preferred produce!

But, presently, such pondering has passed. The present perspective is that Paleo is popular. So, let's present, for your pleasure, the pot roast. So particularly pleasant. So pleasingly plump. So downright delicious!

—Greg

TOTAL TIME: 3 hours, 30 minutes | **VESSEL:** 6 qt Dutch oven | **SERVES:** 6–8

3 lb beef chuck roast
2 tsp salt
½ tsp pepper
2 Tbsp oil
2 onions, sliced into ¼-inch strips
6 cloves garlic
1 Tbsp tomato paste
1½ cups red wine
½ tsp dried thyme
2 bay leaves
½ cup water
4 carrots, peeled and cut into 2-inch pieces
1 pound baby potatoes, cut in half
16 pearl onions, peeled

Preheat the oven to 325°F.

Season the roast by rubbing it with the salt and pepper.

Heat oil in a Dutch oven over medium-high heat. When the oil begins to shimmer, add the roast. Fry for 3 to 5 minutes, until medium-brown. Flip and fry the other side. Remove the roast.

Add the onions and sauté for 6 to 8 minutes, until they begin to brown. Add the whole cloves of garlic and the tomato paste. Stir to coat the onions with the tomato paste, and continue to sauté for another 1 to 2 minutes, until the tomato paste becomes fragrant. Pour in the wine, scraping the bottom of the Dutch oven for any delicious brown bits that might have stuck there. Stir in thyme and bay leaves and turn off the heat.

Add the roast back into the Dutch oven, making sure that it is sitting on the bottom, and not on a pile of onions. The roast should be about ½ covered with liquid. If it isn't, add ½ to 1 cup of water to bring it to the right height. Cover and place it in the oven for 2 hours.

After 2 hours, remove the roast from the oven. Uncover, and place the carrots, potatoes, and pearl onions around the outside of the roast. Cover and place back in the oven for one hour.

Remove the roast and, using two forks, shred it into large, serving-size pieces. Serve with the gravy and veggies from the pot.

Chapter 2
STEWS

Mexiterranean Mess

A cross-continental onion stew

Is fusion cuisine still a thing? I mean, it *was* a thing, and restaurants colorfully blended Country A's formats with Country B's larder; Region X's methods with Region Y's spices. Where brick-and-mortar fusion joints seems to largely be a thing of the past, food trucks have certainly picked up where they left off and continue to innovate in the space. Korean tacos! Chinese pancakes! Cajun fondue! Ethiopian pizza! But still, the trend appears to limit itself to starch from Place 1 with adornments from Place 2, no?

What if fusion cooking was a true, balanced blend of cultures and palates? What if the genius combination of culinary traditions wasn't tidy, walkable, and expected? What if the best flavor elements from two distinct pins on the map came together and turn out to have been a match made in heaven the whole time? I'm not sure you're even ready for this, but here we offer Mexico and the Mediterranean in one heaping, steamy, sloppy spoonful.

—Greg

TOTAL TIME: 1 hour, 15 minutes | **VESSEL:** 6 qt Dutch oven | **SERVES:** 6–8

- 1 cup extra-virgin olive oil
- 3 large Maui, Vidalia, or other sweet onion, large-diced
- 2 tsp kosher salt, divided
- 1 cup kalamata olives, pitted
- 4 cups cherry tomatoes
- 5 cloves garlic, roughly chopped
- 2 Tbsp dried oregano
- 1 Tbsp ground cumin
- 1 Tbsp smoked paprika
- 1 Tbsp ground ancho or other medium-hot chile
- 1 tsp ground black pepper
- 2 (15-oz) cans black beans with their liquid
- 1 (4-oz) can chopped green chiles
- 1 bunch cilantro, roughly chopped

Preheat the oven to 425°F.

Heat oil in a Dutch oven over medium-high heat. When the oil begins to shimmer, add onions and 1 teaspoon of salt and sauté, stirring occasionally, for 15 to 20 minutes, or until the onions are softened and have begun to brown slightly.

Add olives, tomatoes, garlic, oregano, spices, and remaining 1 teaspoon of salt to the pot and stir in evenly. Transfer the pot to the oven and roast for 30 minutes. Carefully remove the pot from the oven. Add beans with their liquid, chiles, and half of the cilantro to the pot, stir in evenly, and transfer the pot back into the oven. Cook for an additional 15 minutes.

Garnish with remaining cilantro to taste and serve hot with Bread Head from page 188, pasta, or rice.

Gentlemen's Gumbo

Enough with the bones and the shells, already!

I *adore* creole gumbo and have cooked so many permutations of the classic stew that it's hard to maintain what "original" may mean or where "authentic" may veer off toward innovation. What exactly *are* the rules? Even though the name derives from an African word for okra, do I have to use it? What color should I make my roux? Lighter for good thickness or darker for more character? Is there a perfect mix of meat and seafood? Do I even mix them? Oddly enough, the most impactful lesson that I've learned about the preparation of gumbo has nothing to do with any question above and comes from an unexpected side of the pond. I picked it up while living in Spain.

The tenet is simple: *Nobody actually wants to eat with their hands*, especially if the dish is ultimately a fork or spoon affair. Who wants to do surgery on delicious shellfish or pick apart a succulent chicken leg, then grab a perfectly clean spoon with gunky fingers? Cooks in Spain, specifically those in Valencia and Catalonia heard the centuries-old cry and created a perfect solution to this issue in the context of paella: Arroz del Senyoret or *Gentlemen's Rice*. Shells and bones done away with ahead of service, ideal for those trying to maintain a gentlemanly posture. Sure, it's more expensive (read: time consuming) and perhaps it loses some dramatic, nay graphic visual appeal, but who cares. One can just get to devouring without messing with a fresh manicure!

—Howie

TOTAL TIME: 2 hours | **VESSEL:** 4–6 qt Dutch oven | **SERVES:** 4–6

- 1 lb shrimp, unpeeled
- 10 oz lobster tails, in shell
- 4 cups All the Bones Broth from page 93, or chicken stock
- 1½ lb chicken thighs, boneless, cut into 1-inch pieces
- 1 tsp ground black pepper
- 2 tsp smoked paprika
- 2 tsp ground cumin
- 1 Tbsp dried oregano
- 1½ tsp salt, divided
- ½ cup butter
- ½ cup all-purpose flour
- 14 oz andouille or other smoked sausage, sliced into ¼-inch rounds
- 1 large onion, diced
- 2 red bell peppers, diced
- 5 ribs celery, thinly sliced
- 4 cloves garlic, roughly chopped
- 1 (15-oz) canned diced tomatoes
- 2 cups frozen okra slices
- 2 scallions, thinly sliced

Remove the shells from the shrimp and lobster. Place the shells in a saucepan with broth or stock. Bring the mixture to a boil, reduce the heat to low, and simmer for 30 minutes. Strain the stock and discard the tails and shells.

(Directions continued on next page)

Preheat the oven to 375°F. In a mixing bowl, combine chicken, pepper, paprika, cumin, oregano, and 1 tsp of salt. Set aside.

Heat a Dutch oven over medium heat. Add butter and flour to the skillet and stir regularly with a wooden spoon every 30 seconds for 10 minutes, or until the roux is the color of milk chocolate.

Add the sausage, onion, bell peppers, celery, and remaining ½ teaspoon of salt to the pot and mix it into the roux. Sauté until the onion is translucent, about 6 to 8 minutes. Add garlic and continue to sauté for an additional minute. Pour in the broth or stock and tomatoes. Increase heat to medium-high and bring the mixture to a boil.

Remove from the heat and add chicken. Cover the pot with a lid and transfer to the oven to braise for 1 hour. Carefully remove the lid, add shrimp and okra, and continue to braise in the oven for 15 minutes, uncovered.

Remove the gumbo from the oven and serve hot with rice and top with scallions.

Cassoulet Américain

A decidedly American twist on a French thing

We Americans *love* our pork and beans. Maybe this magical mixture evokes childhood memories of the classic beanie weenie or perhaps bacon-studded campfire baked beans. I think the latter was my first visit to hog heaven. You know, it could also be that pork and beans are just a natural pairing, like peanut butter and chocolate or pineapple and pizza. I'm kidding. Or am I? As much as we believe that pork and beans is an American love affair, I believe the French created the perfect expression of the dynamic duo in cassoulet. Though, my first cassoulet in France was a bit of an unexpected diamond in the rough.

I travel for food, and my highly anticipated visit to Paris was supposed to serve as some pinnacle of gastronomic pleasure, right? Well, that didn't happen. Perhaps it was the weather and some basic bad choices, but my food experience started with a thud followed with a fizzle then a drizzle. Well, more of a torrent. Despite clearly being off my foodie game, I was really looking forward to a visit to the Basilica of the Sacred Heart and strolling through the hillsides of Montmartre. A morning sprinkle that stood to dissipate only got heavier and heavier until it was the hardest sustained rain I've ever felt. My very soul was wet . . . and hungry.

My soaking family and I took shelter in a crowded brasserie. By this point, a bit gun-shy but hopeful, my kids ordered steak frites, my wife boeuf bourguignon, and I, cassoulet. The place was warm, toasty, and cozy, and I bet on a poetic chance the dish of beans, pork belly and shoulder, sausages, and duck confit would, at worst, hit the spot. Friends, my tummy was finally in the France of storybooks, er, cookbooks. I was overcome with satisfaction. But, considering how France had been treating me up to this point, my mind reeled on how to Americanize this wonderful casserole. Here you go.

—Howie

TOTAL TIME: 3 hours, 30 minutes | **VESSEL:** 4½+ qt Dutch oven | **SERVES:** 6–8

FOR THE TOPPING:

8 oz bread crumbs, ideally fresh
2 tsp kosher salt, divided
7 cloves garlic, minced, divided
1 bunch parsley, chopped, divided

FOR THE CASSEROLE:

4 Tbsp extra-virgin olive oil, divided
4 chicken thighs, bone-in, skin-on
6 fresh pork sausages
6 oz bacon, diced
1 small onion, diced
3 ribs celery, diced
1 red bell pepper, diced
2 tsp smoked paprika
2 tsp ground cumin
1 tsp ground black pepper
2 Tbsp tomato paste
2 (15-oz) cans red kidney beans, with their liquid
2 cups water

(Directions on page 47)

Preheat the oven to 325°F.

In a food processor or blender, thoroughly blend bread crumbs, ½ teaspoon of salt, 4 cloves of garlic, ½ cup of parsley, and 2 tablespoons of olive oil. Set aside.

Add 2 tablespoons of olive oil to a Dutch oven over medium-high heat. Sprinkle the chicken thighs with ½ teaspoon of salt. When the oil begins to shimmer, brown the sausages and chicken in batches until well colored on all sides, about 3 to 6 minutes per batch. Set the meat aside.

Add bacon to the pot and sauté until well browned, about 6 to 8 minutes. Add onion, celery, and bell pepper and continue to sauté until the onion is translucent, about 8 to 10 minutes. Add paprika, cumin, black pepper, the remaining 1 teaspoon of salt, and 3 cloves of minced garlic and continue to sauté for 1 minute.

Stir in tomato paste and continue to sauté for 2 minutes. Stir in beans with their liquid and 2 cups of water.

Into the mixture in the pot, nestle sausages and chicken. Sprinkle the entire surface generously with seasoned bread crumbs. Transfer the pot to the oven and braise for 2½ hours.

Remove the cassoulet from the oven and serve heaping, steaming, piles of beans and meat to lucky guests. A hunk of Bread Head from page 188 or other crusty loaf wouldn't hurt, either!

Faux-joada

The vegan on-ramp to Brazil's national dish

I have a very good friend named Alex, an anthropologist whose laser focus is on Brazil. At some point, he dug deep into the punk rock scene in Sao Paolo. Naturally, he fell in love with the country's national dish, feijoada. A *hard-core* dish. Ha. This delectable slow-cooked concoction of black beans, cured meat, and fresh meat is the soul of Brazil on a plate. Importantly, Alex has also had a lifelong friendship with extreme outdoor adventures fraught with bouts of river-water bacteria, which has rendered him unable to digest meat. What of his love for feijoada? Oh no!

That's where I come into the picture. Alex and I have been trying to formulate and replicate the visceral effect of a protein-heavy, umami-packed alternative design for feijoada for many, many years. Finally, we settled on an unsurprisingly delicious, effective base of soy sauce, tomato paste, sun-dried tomatoes, and caramelized onions with a deep, fun pop of cherry tomatoes, and sweet potatoes for body. Sure, it doesn't provide the meaty heft of real feijoada, but it is a ton healthier. This dish is by no means a diet plan, but it hits all the right notes. It's a mosh pit in your mouth. *Wait*. That doesn't sound right.

—Howie

TOTAL TIME: 1 hour, 15 minutes | **VESSEL:** 5–6 qt Dutch oven | **SERVES:** 8–10

- 2/3 cup extra-virgin olive oil
- 2 large onions, sliced into ¼-inch strips
- 2 tsp kosher salt, divided
- 1 sweet potato, diced
- 4 cups cherry tomatoes
- 4 oz sun-dried tomatoes, thinly sliced
- 3 cloves garlic, roughly chopped
- 3 Tbsp tomato paste
- 2 Tbsp smoked paprika
- 2 tsp ground black pepper
- 4 (15-oz) cans black beans, with their liquid
- 3 Tbsp soy sauce
- 2 cups vegetable broth
- 1 bunch parsley, roughly chopped, divided

Preheat the oven to 425°F.

Heat oil in a Dutch oven over medium heat. When the oil begins to shimmer, add onions and 1 teaspoon of salt, and sauté, stirring occasionally, for 12 to 15 minutes, or until the onions are softened and have begun to brown slightly.

Add sweet potato, tomatoes, sun-dried tomatoes, garlic, tomato paste, paprika, pepper, and remaining salt to the pot and stir in evenly. Transfer the pot to the oven and roast for 25 minutes. Carefully remove the pot from the oven. Add beans with their liquid, soy sauce, broth, and half of the parsley, stir in evenly, and transfer the pot back into the oven. Cook for an additional 20 minutes.

Remove pot from the oven and let it rest for 10 minutes. Scoop directly to bowls, and garnish with remaining parsley. Traditionally, this dish is served with rice, sautéed greens, and sometimes wedges of orange.

What If the Dumplings Stayed Dry?

An opinionated fix for classic chicken stew

Where corned beef hash is my quality test for any diner I run into above the Mason-Dixon line, biscuits and gravy is easily my vehicle of restaurant judgment across the South. There is just something palate-pleasing about the juxtaposition of crispy-flaky-toasty against creamy-savory-meaty that makes me happy and the dish is a fair representative of the skills inside that kitchen. Among dishes that directly pair a starch with something saucy, biscuits and gravy wins in all categories. Why am I rattling on about the queen of Southern diner breakfasts ahead of a recipe for chicken and dumplings? Because, chicken and dumplings has a thing or three to learn from biscuits and gravy!

I do love a steamy bowl of stew that screams the essence of chicken and doesn't pretend to be anything else. But, when dumplings are introduced into the mix, I deeply wish the server just brought some fantastic chicken brew with a side of biscuits! Any way you cut it, flour dumplings that cook in the stew itself often become gummy and generally fail to raise the stew to more than one note. Biscuits, on the other hand, whether smothered or dunked-in, bring a whole new level of enjoyment for the mouth and retain that crispy-flaky-toasty character mentioned above. Just like me in a diner, hold your judgment until after you eat. Then, tell *everyone* I was right.

—Howie

TOTAL TIME: 1 hour, 30 minutes | **VESSEL:** 4–6 qt Dutch oven | **SERVES:** 8–10

- 5 Tbsp extra-virgin olive oil, divided
- 1 large onion, diced
- 4 ribs celery, diced
- 1 large carrot, diced
- 2 tsp kosher salt, divided
- 2 Tbsp all-purpose flour
- 1 tsp ground black pepper
- 8 cups water
- 4–5 lb chicken, cut into 8 pieces
- 1 cup frozen peas
- ½ bunch parsley, roughly chopped, divided
- 1 recipe The Pot Lid Can Do That? biscuit dough from page 208, uncooked

Add 2 tablespoons olive oil to a Dutch oven over medium heat. Add onion, celery, carrot, and 1 teaspoon of salt and sauté for 8 to 10 minutes, or until the onion is beginning to brown. Add flour and continue to sauté for 1 minute. Add pepper, water, and chicken pieces and increase the heat to medium-high. Bring the mixture to a boil, reduce the heat to low, and cover with a lid. Simmer for 45 minutes.

Preheat the oven to 400°F.

Uncover the pot and transfer the chicken to a cutting board. When the chicken has cooled, pull the meat into bite-size shreds. Add the cooked chicken back into the pot, along with the frozen peas and half of the parsley.

Wipe the lid dry of condensation. Grease the underside of the lid with 1 tablespoon of olive oil. Cut out dough rounds with a 3-inch biscuit cutter or the top of a 3-inch wide glass. Place the dough rounds on top of the flipped lid, butting up against each other, to fit as many as possible. Place the remainder on a greased sheet pan. Drizzle 2 remaining tablespoons of olive oil over the biscuit dough.

Transfer the otherwise filled Dutch oven with the lid on upside down to the oven and bake until biscuits are starting to brown, about 20 to 25 minutes. Remove the pot from the oven and serve the biscuits with hot, thankfully non-gooey stew, topped with remaining parsley.

Those Beans from That Mexican Place

Like Boston baked beans with a different accent

We all know the scenario. You and your friends just ate *big* at the local Tex-Mex restaurant and the reviews are bandied about on the long walk home. "Man, those veggie enchiladas were awesome!" "Did you see the size of my chimichanga? Enormous!" "The beef fajitas were some of the best I've ever had!" But, what if you pulled out, "those beans, dude, hella fly, crazy good!" It would sound weird, right? Everyone would stop in their tracks and run away from you, though maybe only due to your 1992 turn of phrase. Restaurant beans too often get the shaft. They need and deserve more love.

No matter your dinner choice, I promise there was more intricate thought and attention paid to the cooking of the beans. Pleasantly creamy, spicy, but not too spicy, meaty but not meat-heavy, deeply flavored but not overwhelming. It took some years of honing this balance, but all in an effort to give simple beans their due. Once you try this and put it up against whatever south-of-the-border masterpiece you're serving tonight, your dinner guests are sure to be yammering on about them on their way out the door. Then, have a margarita on me. I'll pay you back, promise.

—Howie

TOTAL TIME: 4 hours, 30 minutes, or overnight plus 2 hours, 30 minutes
VESSEL: 5–6 qt Dutch oven | **SERVES:** 8–10

- 1 lb dried pinto beans
- 16 cups water, divided
- 3 Tbsp extra-virgin olive oil
- 1 onion, diced
- 5 cloves garlic, lightly crushed
- 3 jalapeño peppers, sliced thinly
- 2 tsp kosher salt
- 1 (14-oz) can crushed tomatoes
- 1 smoked ham hock or smoked turkey drumstick
- ½ bunch cilantro, roughly chopped, divided
- Queso fresco and pico de gallo, for garnish

Place dried beans in a large bowl and cover with 10 cups of water. Let it sit on the counter overnight.

OR, Preheat the oven to 400°F, then place dried beans in a Dutch oven and cover with 10 cups of water. Cover the pot and transfer to the oven for 2 hours. Remove the pot from the oven, carefully uncover, and drain the beans. Empty and wipe out the pot.

Heat oil in the Dutch oven over medium-high heat. When the oil begins to shimmer, add onion and sauté, stirring occasionally, for 8 to 10 minutes, or until the onion is softened and has begun to brown slightly. Add garlic, jalapeños, and salt and continue to sauté for 3 to 4 minutes or until very fragrant.

Add tomatoes, ham hock or turkey drumstick, half of the cilantro, drained beans, and 6 cups of water. Increase the temperature to medium-high and bring to a boil. Remove from the heat, cover, and transfer the pot to the oven and braise for 1 hour. Carefully remove the lid and check a bean to see if they are fully cooked. Leave the lid off and continue to braise for 30 minutes to 1 hour, or until it has reached the desired creamy consistency. As needed, add water ½ cup at a time to keep the beans from drying out.

Remove from the oven, and remove the ham hock or turkey drumstick from the pot. Pick the meat off, mix into the beans or serve on the side. Serve beans with some rice, and garnish with remaining cilantro, cheese, and/or pico de gallo.

Sichuan "Water-Boiled" Fish

The name is, like, the opposite of the dish

The Chinese naming convention for dishes is often fantastical (Buddha jumps over a wall), sometimes brutally literal (stinky tofu), and occasionally, it's just plain cruel and sarcastic. Such is the case for *water-boiled* fish. It was the first time Howie and I were in Chengdu, the capital of Sichuan Province. We stopped over in town for a few days to enjoy what was about to be a cross-China phenemonon—Sichuan cuisine. Sichuan's reputation was well known as the hot-headed home of scorchingly spicy food, so we were forewarned. As we sat down at the first decent looking hole-in-the-wall joint we ran across and readied ourselves for an onslaught of capsicum, we had no idea what was about to unfold.

We naturally order up the classics, kung pao chicken, mapo tofu, and in reviewing the voluminous menu, decided to get something that appeared to be on the calmer side, perhaps even soothing. *Water-boiled fish* seemed tame, maybe boring, but potentially cooling. What came out of the kitchen, bubbling, hissing, and spewing lava was anything but tame, far from soothing, and the opposite of cooling. The expected heat from dried red chiles was only the beginning of the taste adventure as the mouth-numbing Sichuan peppercorn sent us running for the fridge for rescue-via-frosty-beverages. Howie, after guzzling freezing cold yet decidedly terrible Chinese beer and wiping his nose, chuckles, "Wow. What kind of water did they use?"

—Greg

TOTAL TIME: 30 minutes | **VESSEL:** 1½+ qt Dutch oven | **SERVES:** 2–3

- 1 lb tilapia fillets, cut into 2-inch pieces
- 1 egg white
- ¾ tsp kosher salt
- ½ tsp ground white pepper
- 1 Tbsp cornstarch
- 2 Tbsp canola or vegetable oil
- 4 scallions, white and green parts separated, thinly sliced
- 4 cloves garlic, minced
- ½ inch ginger, minced
- 3 Tbsp chile-garlic sauce, or other chile paste
- ½ tsp ground Sichuan peppercorn (optional)
- 3 cups water
- 2 cups shredded lettuce
- Sesame seeds for garnish

In a mixing bowl, thoroughly combine fish pieces, egg white, salt, pepper, and cornstarch. Set aside for 20 minutes.

Add oil to a Dutch oven over medium-high heat. When the oil begins to shimmer, quickly sauté scallion whites, garlic, and ginger for 1 minute. Stir in chile sauce or paste and Sichuan pepper, if using, and continue to sauté for 2 minutes.

Pour in water, then add fish pieces one at a time. Bring the mixture to a boil and immediately turn off the heat.

Prepare a heatproof serving vessel by laying a bed of shredded lettuce. Carefully pour or ladle the fish stew over the lettuce and garnish with scallion greens and sesame seeds. Serve immediately with some rice and a veggie for good measure!

Is it Vegan–Cajun or Cajun–Vegan?

Shockingly good red beans and rice

I am not vegan. I am not vegetarian. I am mostly pescatarian, but occasionally I eat meat. That being said, I always eat *delicious* food, and I don't discriminate or eschew the vegan section of the menu because I think it's somehow less-than. When I cook, particularly when I am developing a recipe, I tend to explore *why* meat is used in this dish or that. More often than not, unless it's a meat-centric dish, meat adds so little that, with a bit of cajoling, it's easily dropped from the playlist. Such is the case with this red beans and rice formula. It's one of those rare dishes that won't convert a carnivore, but it certainly gives one pause and inspires reexamination of one's entire eating landscape. It's *that* good.

Traditional red beans and rice was a Monday dish across Cajun country, since Sunday dinner was all about the ham. Braising beans with the leftover hambone the next day was an obvious way to reduce waste and make the beans delish. I agree that hambone-infused legumes can be otherworldly, but when I began to break down *why* they were so good, alternatives became clear. Smokey, check; the occasional chew, check; deep umami satisfaction, check; unctuous mouthfeel, check. It's stunning what a little liquid smoke, sun-dried tomatoes, soy sauce, and the magical liquid from a can of beans can do. Living *high on the hog*, indeed.

—Howie

TOTAL TIME: 1 hour, 20 minutes | **VESSEL:** 3+ qt Dutch oven | **SERVES:** 4–6

3 Tbsp extra-virgin olive oil
3 scallions, white and green parts separated, thinly sliced
3 ribs celery, diced
1 green bell pepper, diced
1 tsp kosher salt
½ tsp ground black pepper
1 tsp adobo or other all-purpose seasoning
1 tsp ground cayenne pepper (optional)
3 cloves garlic, minced
2 oz sun-dried tomatoes, minced
3 Tbsp tomato paste
3 Tbsp soy sauce
½ tsp liquid smoke
2 (15-oz) cans red kidney beans, with their liquid
2 cups vegetable stock or water
Cooked white rice for serving

Add olive oil to a Dutch oven over medium heat. When the oil begins shimmering, add scallion whites, celery, bell pepper, salt, and spices, and sauté until the vegetables are very soft, about 10 to 12 minutes. Stir in garlic, sun-dried tomatoes, tomato paste, soy sauce, and liquid smoke and sauté for an additional 3 minutes.

Pour in beans with their liquid and stock or water. Increase the heat to medium-high and bring to a boil. Reduce the heat to low and simmer the beans for 1 hour.

Serve the beans with steamy white rice and a garnish of scallion greens. *Laissez les bon temps rouler!*

Non Dago Nire Marmitako?

Basque tuna and potato stew

Before moving to Spain, I was in the same boat as many Americans who assume the streets are a festival of moving feasts, lined with sizzling paella pans, roaming pitchers of sangria, and fluffy potato omelets being Frisbee'ed through the air. This rather ridiculous and delicious-sounding illustration is not far off from my naive misconception of one of the world's consistently under-sung cuisines. Upon arriving in my new home of Barcelona, however, the most surprising revelation wasn't the diversity of excellent rice dishes or the magic simplicity that is tortilla Española. The real culinary shock, the surprising queen of the menu, the stuff of culinary legend seems more at home in a sushi bar than a tapas bar. Yes, Spain is having an unquestionably quixotic and passionate affair with *tuna*—the rarer the better!

I set upon a mesmerizing quest to explore the dizzying array of tuna preparations around the Catalan capital. It was a delicious year and a half. Just when I thought the results were in and I could write a dissertation on the topic, along would come another permutation of tuna, cut and treated in yet another unique way. Trust me, it was the best kind of unfinished feeling. Months into the journey, I had eaten my weight in yellowfin, bluefin, and albacore, and enjoyed enough exquisite versions of tataki, tartare, and sashimi that would make the Japanese proud. Then . . . I spent a few weeks in San Sebastian, Basque Country, which tipped the scales toward utterly ridiculous. I may write volumes one day, but here's a highlight: cubes of barely seared yellowfin, topped with tranches of grilled foie gras and severely reduced soy sauce . . .

But, since this is a Dutch oven cookbook and most of these outlandish tuna dishes don't come from a Dutch oven, I'll share one that does. Frankly, it placed a close second during my stay in San Sebastian. Enjoy.

—Howie

TOTAL TIME: 25 minutes | **VESSEL:** 3+ qt Dutch oven | **SERVES:** 4–6

- 1 lb tuna steaks, cut into 1-inch cubes
- 1½ tsp kosher salt, divided
- 2 Tbsp extra-virgin olive oil
- 1 onion, diced
- 1 red bell pepper, diced
- 4 cloves garlic, minced
- 1 large tomato, grated, skin discarded
- 1 (4-oz) can green chiles (hot or mild)
- 1 russet potato, peeled, large-diced
- 4 cups fish or chicken stock

In a mixing bowl, combine tuna and ½ teaspoon of salt and set aside.

Add olive oil to a Dutch oven over medium heat. When the oil begins to shimmer, add onion and sauté until soft, about 4 to 6 minutes. Add bell pepper and garlic and continue to sauté for 3 minutes. Stir in grated tomato and chiles and allow it to reduce for 2 minutes. Add potato and stock, increase the heat to medium-high, and bring to a boil. Reduce the heat to low, cover the pot with a lid, and simmer until the potatoes are cooked through, about 9 to 11 minutes.

Remove the lid and stir in the tuna. Replace the lid and continue to simmer for 1 to 2 minutes, or until the tuna is barely cooked on the surface.

Turn off the heat and serve steamy, chunky, Basque-y goodness with Bread Head from page 188, another crusty bread.

Actual Pumpkin-Flavored Curry

"Pumpkin spice" has nothing to do with pumpkin

Have you *ever had* pumpkin? *No,* not pumpkin cake, pumpkin coffee, pumpkin bread, or pumpkin cookies. Pumpkin. It's delicious and has nothing to do with cinnamon, cloves, ginger, and nutmeg. The taste of pumpkin is actually closer to that of a sweet potato or acorn squash than a sticky bun. The fruit itself plays a better savory hero than it ever will a sweet. Why don't we as a society start to call the craze what is really is: *Pumpkin PIE Spice fill-in-the-blank!*

Notably, Southern Indian cooks have been working with winter squash decidedly longer than your local barista has been frothing "pumpkin spice" lattes. Applications run the gamut of Indian cuisine: Tandoor oven roasted squash, squash dumplings, squash-filled samosa, and yes, as stereotypical as it may seem, squash curry. If this recipe doesn't convince you that the latte you drank this morning should never mess with the word *pumpkin,* nothing will.

—Greg

TOTAL TIME: 30 minutes | **VESSEL:** 3–5 qt Dutch oven | **SERVES:** 4–6

2 Tbsp ghee or extra-virgin olive oil
1 large onion, diced
4 cloves garlic, roughly chopped
1 inch ginger, minced
1 tsp kosher salt
1 tsp ground cardamom
1 tsp ground turmeric
1 tsp ground cumin
1 (13-oz) can coconut cream
1 (13.5-oz) can coconut milk
1 cup water
6 oz baby spinach
1–1½ lb pumpkin or butternut squash peeled, seeded, large diced
Toasted cashews and lime wedges for garnish

Add oil to a Dutch oven over medium heat. When the oil begins to shimmer, add onion and sauté until translucent, about 6 to 8 minutes. Add garlic, ginger, salt, cardamom, turmeric, and cumin and continue to sauté for 2 minutes. Stir in coconut cream, coconut milk, and water, increase the heat to medium-high, and bring to a boil.

Stir in spinach until it all wilts. Reduce the heat to low and add pumpkin or squash. Cover and cook until the squash is soft, about 10 to 12 minutes.

Remove the cover and serve hot alongside rice or naan bread, garnished with cashews and lime wedges for squeezing. Perhaps, serve this dish alongside Lamb Vindaloo from page 71 and An Eggplant and Tomato Love Story from page 73.

Meat and Potatoes, Japanese Style

It's what to eat in Japan when you don't eat fish

You may have noticed that Howie does all our fish recipes. This is not a coincidence. Much to my culinary chagrin, I've never developed a taste for fish or seafood. Which is a shame. Unless, of course, your mother-in-law is a flounder, in which case, preferring chicken earns you a few points.

Enjoying Japan while not eating fish has led me on many a culinary adventure. While you are focused on sushi, I'm enjoying a curry donut. While you're risking your life eating blowfish, I'm sitting at a yakitori bar. While you're on your fourth tuna hand roll, I'm enjoying *nikujaga!*

What is nikujaga, you ask? It's an amazingly quick stew made of thinly sliced beef braised with potatoes and vegetables in a sweet and rich broth. Give it a try. You won't be sorry.

—Greg

TOTAL TIME: 30 min | **VESSEL:** 3 qt Dutch oven | **SERVES:** 3–4

- 2 Tbsp vegetable or canola oil
- 1 small onion, thinly sliced
- 1 carrot, sliced into ¼-inch-thick rounds
- 8 baby potatoes, cut in half
- 1 lb beef filet, sliced thinly
- 2 cups water
- ½ lb green beans, tips snapped off
- 2 Tbsp granulated sugar
- 1 tsp kosher salt
- 6 Tbsp soy sauce
- 4 Tbsp sake or dry sherry
- 4 Tbsp mirin

Heat oil in a Dutch oven over medium-high heat. When the oil begins to shimmer, add the onion, carrot, and potatoes, and sauté for 4 to 5 minutes, until the onions begin to soften. Add the beef and continue to sauté until the beef is light brown, about 2 to 3 minutes. Add the water, bring it to a boil, and lower the heat to a light simmer. Cover and allow to simmer for 15 minutes.

Add the green beans to the pot, along with the sugar, salt, soy sauce, sake or sherry, and mirin. Cover and allow to simmer until the green beans are cooked through, about 8 minutes. Serve immediately over rice.

California Dreamin' Chili

A vegan dream in stew form

As a proud third-generation Californian, I embody and celebrate most of our stereotypes. Been arrested at a sit-in? *Twice*. Enjoy tofu? *Love it*. Use the word "like" more than is, like, totally necessary? *Like, yeah!* But you don't need to be a Californian to enjoy this vegan chili. In fact, I must confess, sometimes we don't even eat this chili on a bed of sprouted quinoa. Don't tell my bros down at the farmers' market, but it is, like, pretty bodacious with *Fritos*.

—Greg

TOTAL TIME: 30 min | **VESSEL:** 3 qt Dutch oven | **SERVES:** 6–8, as a side dish

1 Tbsp oil
1 onion, chopped
1 tsp salt
1 green pepper, diced
1 jalapeño, seeds removed, and minced
6 cloves garlic, minced
2 tsp cumin
2 tsp sweet paprika
3 Tbsp chile powder
1 cup water
24 oz. can of black beans, drained
2 zucchini, diced
½ cup cilantro

Heat oil in a Dutch oven over medium-high heat. When the oil begins to shimmer, add the onion and salt, and sauté for 6 to 8 minutes, until the onion begins to brown. Add the green pepper, jalapeño, and garlic, and continue to sauté for 2 to 3 minutes. Next, add the cumin, paprika, and chile powder, and stir to combine. Fry for another 30 seconds, until fragrant.

Add the water, black beans, and zucchini. Bring to a boil, and lower the heat to a simmer. Allow to simmer, uncovered, for 20 minutes, or until the zucchini is fully cooked. Serve topped with cilantro.

A Peking Duck Gets Lost in Texas

Spoiler: He ends up in a chili bowl

A few years back, Greg and I produced a Web series called *Sauced in Translation* in which I traveled around China cooking American food inspired by local dishes. When we visited Chengdu, the spicy capital of Sichuan Province, I was blown away by the quality of the available meats and of course, the hot chiles. Naturally, I decided to make chili con carne for an adoring streetside crowd. The local twist was my use of soybeans, halal beef, dried and fresh peppers, and Chengdu's infamous Snow beer. The stew went over so well that several townies asked me what Chinese dish I was making the next day! *My chili passed as Chinese food*. How 'bout that!

Ever since shooting that series, I've wondered what would happen if I turned the tables and traveled the United States cooking Chinese dishes based on American favorites. Would I end up in a similar place, recipe-wise? This chili is an ode to these cross-culinary-cultural thoughts, in which I specifically ponder if the Peking duck experience could be enjoyed with a spoon rather than a pair of chopsticks. Except for the bacon-esque crispy skin heralded across Beijing, I think I hit the nail on the head.

—Howie

TOTAL TIME: 40 minutes | **VESSEL:** 3+ qt Dutch oven | **SERVES:** 3–4

- 2 Tbsp extra-virgin olive oil
- 3 scallions, thinly sliced
- 4 cloves garlic, minced
- ½ inch ginger, minced
- 3 jalapeño peppers, thinly sliced
- 1 lb duck breasts, boneless, skin removed, or ground duck meat
- 1 tsp kosher salt
- 2–3 chipotle peppers in adobo, minced
- 1 (4-oz) can green chiles (hot or mild)
- 2 Tbsp hoisin sauce
- 2 Tbsp all-purpose flour
- 3 cups chicken stock
- 1 scallion, julienned, for garnish

Add oil to a Dutch oven over medium-high heat. When the oil begins to shimmer, add scallions, garlic, ginger, and jalapeños, and quickly sauté for 2 minutes. Add duck and salt and continue to sauté until the meat is no longer pink, about 3 to 4 minutes.

Stir in chipotles, green chiles, and hoisin and continue to sauté for 1 minute. Sprinkle flour atop the mixture and continue to sauté for 2 minutes. Pour in stock, stir, and bring to a boil. Reduce the heat to low, place a lid on the pot, and simmer for 30 minutes.

Serve with a garnish of julienned scallions and some tortilla chips, over some rice or some buttery corn bread.

Curry. No, Chili! No, Curry!

It's both and neither

Food words can be confusing, but they don't have to be. *Curry* is a flavorful herb leaf that is widely used in South Indian cooking. Curry is not the name of a dish. Or rather, it wasn't the name of a dish until people got lazy. The English were so enamored of the dishes they encountered when they, er, hung out in India that they invented a spice mix that hit all the highlights: cumin, coriander, clove, turmeric, black pepper, etc. They generically and unceremoniously enshrined Indian-style stews under this errant *curry* label. Even the name *curry* is probably wrong, as the English are likely to have misappropriated and used the Southern Indian word *kari*, which means sauce. Nothing to do with the herb.

Chili (or more properly *chile*) is a pepper pod that often carries some spicy heat. Chili is not the name of a dish. Or rather, it wasn't the name of a dish until people got lazy. Southern Texan cattlemen were so enamored of the dishes they encountered when they, er, hung out in Northern Mexico that they took a "to go" box. It was actually pretty inventive. Beef, chiles, and herbs were pressed into cakes and dried, ready for rehydrating on the trail. But they lazily called "chile con carne" *chili,* thus forever confusing what is called what.

We have the English and Texans to thank for these confusions, I suppose. Even though the dish names are confusing, they have developed, over time, a shared meaning. I guess that's what language is. Oh well. Now, you get to decide whether presented below is a curry or a chili.

—Greg

TOTAL TIME: 1 hours, 20 minutes | **VESSEL:** 4½+ qt Dutch oven | **SERVES:** 6–8

FOR THE CHILI/CURRY:

3 Tbsp ghee or extra-virgin olive oil
1 large onion, minced
6 cloves garlic, minced
1 inch ginger, minced
2 jalapeño peppers, thinly sliced
1 lb ground ground turkey or chicken
1 tsp kosher salt
1 tsp ground turmeric
1 tsp ground cumin
1–2 tsp ground cayenne (optional)
2 (15-oz) cans chickpeas, with their liquid
1 (15-oz) can crushed tomatoes
2 cups chicken stock

FOR THE RAITA:

1½ cup Greek-style yogurt
½ cup mint leave, loosely packed, plus more for garnish
½ tsp ground cumin
¼ tsp kosher salt

(Directions on next page)

Add ghee or oil to a Dutch oven over medium-high heat. When the oil begins to shimmer, add onion, garlic, ginger, and jalapeños, and sauté until the texture is that of a paste, about 5 to 7 minutes. Add meat and spices and continue to sauté until the meat is no longer pink, about 3 to 4 minutes. Stir in chickpeas, their liquid, tomatoes, and stock, stir throughout, and bring to a boil. Reduce the heat to low and simmer for 1 hour.

In a blender or food processor, puree raita ingredients, leaving some whole mint leaves for garnish.

Serve the curry chili with a dollop of raita and a few mint leaves over some rice or with a toasty flatbread.

Lamb Vindaloo

Ah, the smell of it

I won't bore you with the fact that this Indian lamb dish was originally a Portuguese pork dish. Wait, I guess I just did. Fine, but I won't tell you that the Portuguese dropped plenty of other culinary gems during their sixteenth-century traipse around the globe, like chiles in China, tempura in Japan, pork adobo in the Philippines, chile verde in Mexico, egg custard in Hong Kong, feijoada in Brazil, salt cod in, well, everywhere else, etc. Oops, did it again! Sorry. I'd rather talk about that famed vindaloo scent.

I am not a particular fan of the smell of vinegar or mustard. But there's something about Indian ingenuity around aroma that piques my interest. Both vinegar and mustard seem to open up the nose to potentially hidden essence within a dish. In other words, where the initial smell of vinegar and/or mustard may be jarring to some (me), after blending with other aromatic elements of a recipe, *those* aromas are the lucky ones that are accentuated. Additionally, the potency of such vapor seems to allow it to linger much longer beyond the cooking event. After an initial gut punch of vinegar and mustard, may a cloud of coconut, garlic, onion, and cumin pervade your lovely home. I'm jealous already.

—Howie

TOTAL TIME: 2 hours, 30 minutes | **VESSEL:** 3–5 qt Dutch oven | **SERVES:** 6–8

1 small onion, quartered
10 cloves garlic, peeled
1 Tbsp red wine vinegar
2 Tbsp grainy mustard
1 Tbsp ground cumin
1 Tbsp ground turmeric
1–2 tsp ground cayenne pepper
1 tsp ground black pepper
2 tsp kosher salt, divided
4 Tbsp extra-virgin olive oil, divided
2 lb lamb shoulder chops, bone-in
1 (13-oz) can coconut cream
1 cup water
1 russet potato, peeled, diced
Cilantro, chopped, for garnish

Preheat the oven to 325°F.

In a food processor or a blender, puree onion, garlic, vinegar, mustard, cumin, turmeric, cayenne, pepper, 1 teaspoon salt, and 2 tablespoons olive oil.

Add remaining 2 tablespoons olive oil to a Dutch oven over medium-high heat. Season lamb chops with remaining 1 teaspoon of salt. In batches, sear lamb chops, 1½ minutes per side and set aside. Add seasoning puree to the hot oil and sauté for 1 minute. Add coconut cream and water, stir to combine, and bring to a boil over medium-high heat. Turn off the heat and add seared lamb to the pot.

Cover with a lid and transfer the pot to the oven and braise for 1 hour, 30 minutes. Carefully remove the pot from the oven and stir in diced potato, cover again, and continue to braise in the oven for 30 minutes.

(Directions continued on next page)

Remove the pot from the oven. Carefully pluck the lamb chops from the sauce and place on a sheet pan. Remove their bones and dice the meat. Stir the lamb meat back into the sauce.

Serve vindaloo with naan bread or rice, garnished with cilantro. You can even serve this dish alongside Actual Pumpkin-Flavored Curry from page 61 and An Eggplant and Tomato Love Story from page 73.

An Eggplant and Tomato Love Story

A fiery Indian affair in a single pot

When I was growing up, I was surrounded by Italians who loved to cook, and eggplant. Lots and lots of eggplant. Like many kids, I steered clear of the stuff, gooey, bitter, seedy. Yuck. Then I moved to China and my world completely changed. The ways in which Chinese cooks were treating it altered my very chemistry. Crispy pork-stuffed eggplant, roasted eggplant and cilantro salad, braised eggplant with the hottest peppers known to humankind. If I listed every permutation and application of eggplant in China, I would have to stop writing this book and my publisher would be disappointed. Note to self: Write Chinese eggplant book.

When I returned to the United States, all of those previously hated eggplant recipes somehow tasted brand new. *Eggplant can be delicious*—when treated right. Beyond my new fascination bordering on obsession with cooking eggplant, I was learning how culinary cultures around the globe handled it and ran into some interesting tidbits.

For example, on many an Indian menu you will find Baingan Bharta, or highly spiced stewed eggplant and tomato. If you're going for a dish that changes the character of all of the players, this is it. The acids in the tomato counter the potential sliminess of the eggplant and make it creamy. The inherent sweetness of both fruits match well and introduce yet a third fruitiness. The spices used accentuate the just-right bitterness. Oh, and as it turns out, eggplant and tomato together are no firewall against Indian-level spice. This dish is hot.

—Howie

TOTAL TIME: 1 hour, 30 minutes | **VESSEL:** 1½–3 qt Dutch oven | **SERVES:** 3–4

1 large or 2 smaller eggplants
3 Tbsp extra-virgin olive oil
1 small red onion, diced
½ inch ginger, minced
4 cloves garlic, minced
½ tsp kosher salt
½ tsp garam masala
1 tsp ground cayenne
½ tsp ground cardamom
¼ tsp ground black pepper
¼ tsp ground cinnamon
1 tomato, halved, grated, skin discarded
1 (4-oz) can diced green chiles, hot or mild
¼ cup water, as needed
Cilantro for garnish

Preheat the oven to 375°F.

Use the tip of a knife to prick the eggplant 10 times. Place the eggplant in the oven and roast for 30 minutes. Flip them over and continue to roast for 30 minutes. Remove from the oven and allow them to cool until they can be handled.

(Directions continued on page 75)

While the eggplant is roasting, add olive oil to a Dutch oven over medium heat. Add onion and sauté until very soft, but not browned, about 20 minutes. Add ginger, garlic, and all spices and continue to sauté for 3 minutes. Stir in grated tomato and chiles.

When the eggplant is cool enough to be handled, cut open lengthwise and scoop out the roasted flesh and discard the skins. Chop the flesh into bite-size chunks and stir into the pot. If the texture is too thick, add water as needed to loosen up the stew. Allow the mixture to come back to serving heat.

Garnish with cilantro and serve hot with naan bread or rice. Maybe pair this dish with Lamb Vindaloo from page 71 and Actual Pumpkin-Flavored Curry from page 61.

Neighborhood Squid Swims in Own Ink

Creamy Spanish black rice with calamari

Paella is the first—and most of the time, only—Spanish rice dish that Americans think of. But, what if I told you that most "paella" recipes are not paella, but appropriate the *word* "paella" to give a dish a stronger identity? "Vegan paella" is *not a thing;* "Creamy paella" must have been cooked wrong; "Chorizo paella?" *That would be crazy*! Spanish chefs are constantly debating paella rules; after all the dish was named for the pan and not a set of ingredients. Still, purists insist that there exists *paella Valenciana* with rabbit, chicken, snails, and beans and *paella de Mariscos* with only seafood. Everything else should just be called *arroz de* something.

Since we're talking opinions, I'll tell you that what goes on top of the rice is the least important aspect of the *arroz de* something versus "paella" nomenclature. What I discovered upon moving to Spain is that the *rice* is the true star of any of these dishes. And it can vary so much. Paella is a "dry" rice dish, which means that all liquid is absorbed or evaporated. Then, things get more interesting. There are a number of levels of "wet" within the Spanish rice landscape—most prominently, *arroz meloso*, or creamy rice, and *arroz caldoso*, or soupy rice. Meloso became my go-to weeknight staple (still is). My kids fell in love with this creepy-looking version colored with squid ink. I think you will, too!

—Howie

TOTAL TIME: 1 hour | **VESSEL:** 3–5 qt Dutch oven | **SERVES:** 6–8

- 1/3 cup extra-virgin olive oil
- 10 oz calamari, 1-cm rings, patted dry
- 1 onion, diced
- 3 cloves garlic, minced
- 1 medium tomato, grated, skin discarded
- 2 tsp smoked paprika
- 2 cups Bomba, arborio ,or other round, short-grain rice
- 6 cups seafood or vegetable stock
- 2 Tbsp dark soy sauce
- 3 oz squid or cuttlefish ink
- 1 Tbsp dried oregano
- ½ tsp kosher salt
- 3 oz piquillo or other roasted red peppers, peeled, seeded, thin strips

Preheat your oven to 350°F.

Heat a Dutch oven over medium-high heat and add the olive oil. When the oil begins to shimmer, add the calamari rings and fry for 2 to 3 minutes, until the calamari begins to color. Reduce the heat to medium and add the onion and sauté for 4 to 6 minutes, until the onion softens. Add the garlic, grated tomato, and smoked paprika, and sauté for an additional 3 to 4 minutes, until the liquid from the tomato has evaporated. Add the rice and continue to sauté for 5 minutes.

Add stock, soy sauce, ink, oregano, and salt to the pot and stir in evenly. Increase the heat to medium-high and bring the mixture to a boil. Cover the pot with a lid and transfer to the oven for 30 minutes. Remove the pot from the oven, remove the lid, and serve bowls of hot black goodness, garnished with a pop of red peppers.

Hachee! Gesundheit!

The only Dutch recipe in the book

Thanks to the kind folks of the Netherlands for offering up not only the single Dutch recipe in this Dutch oven cookbook, but potentially the simplest, most delicious stew I've ever cooked. Beef. Onions. Garlic. Time.

Thanks also to the kind folks of the Netherlands for naming it Hachee. That's a lot of fun to say. Try not to smile. It's impossible.

—Greg

TOTAL TIME: 3 hours, 30 minutes | **VESSEL:** 4½–6 qt Dutch oven | **SERVES:** 6–8

- ¼ cup extra-virgin olive oil
- 2 tsp kosher salt, divided
- 1½–2 lb beef chuck roast, cut into 1-inch pieces
- 2 large onions, sliced into ¼-inch strips
- 6 cloves garlic, lightly crushed
- ¼ cup all-purpose flour
- 4 cups beef or chicken stock
- 2 cloves

Preheat the oven to 325°F.

Add olive oil to a Dutch oven over medium-high heat. Massage 1 teaspoon of salt into the meat pieces. In batches, brown the beef, about 3 minutes per batch, and using a slotted spoon, set aside.

Reduce the heat to medium, add onions to the pot, and sauté until translucent and beginning to brown, about 8 to 10 minutes Add garlic and continue to sauté for 1 minute. Sprinkle flour over the mixture and sauté for 2 additional minutes.

Pour in stock, add seared beef pieces, and stir to combine. Add cloves, remove from the heat, cover with a lid, and transfer to the oven to braise for 2½ hours.

Carefully remove the lid and continue to braise for 30 minutes.

Remove the pot from the oven and serve this Dutch masterpiece with rice or "Scalloped" Potatoes Bother Us from page 141.

Ratatouille

Even better than the movie

Just like the animated film about a rat who secretly cooks by controlling the limbs of a bumbling chef-in-training, I love the namesake dish, ratatouille! What I don't love is the disparity between the humble Provençal countryside version and the uppity urban version. The former generally yields a mountain of mushy vegetables that largely lose their character. The latter, as you may have seen during the last scenes of the animated movie is an intricate, gorgeous spiral of the most laborious, time-consuming food you will ever cook. What's a cook without a rodent partner to do?

This recipe blends the best of both worlds. It allows hearty vegetables that can stand up on their own, like eggplant, peppers, and onions to collude in a stew-like fashion. But it also invites comparatively delicate vegetables like tomatoes and zucchini to just sort of hang outside of the fray and get roasted, bathing in olive oil. Sounds nice, doesn't it? It doesn't hurt that the dish is also as beautiful as any offering in Paris without the airfare or the creepy mimes.

—Greg

TOTAL TIME: 45 minutes | **VESSEL:** 1½ qt Dutch oven | **SERVES:** 3–4

- ½ cup extra-virgin olive oil, divided
- 1 small eggplant, diced
- 1 tsp kosher salt, divided
- 1 small red onion, sliced into ⅛-inch strips
- 1 roasted red bell pepper, peeled and seeded, diced
- 2 Tbsp tomato paste
- ½ tsp ground black pepper
- 1 tsp fresh thyme leaves, or ½ tsp dried
- 1 small zucchini, sliced into ⅛-inch rounds
- 2 Roma tomatoes, sliced into ⅛-inch rounds

Preheat the oven to 375°F.

Add ¼ cup of olive oil to a Dutch oven over medium heat. When the oil begins to shimmer, add eggplant and ½ teaspoon of salt and sauté until the eggplant is soft and begins to brown, about 4 to 6 minutes. Remove cooked eggplant from the pot.

Add 2 tablespoons of olive oil. When the oil begins to shimmer, add onion and sauté until they are translucent, about 6 to 8 minutes. Add roasted pepper and tomato paste, stir in, and continue to sauté for 2 minutes. Remove the pot from the heat and stir in cooked eggplant, black pepper, and thyme. With the back of a spoon, press the top of the mixture flat.

Add zucchini and tomato rounds to the top of the mixture in the pot in an overlapping style, like roof tiles. Sprinkle the tomatoes and zucchini with ½ teaspoon of salt and drizzle with 2 tablespoons of olive oil. Transfer the pot to the oven and roast until the vegetables on top are just beginning to gain color, about 20 to 25 minutes.

Remove the ratatouille from the oven and serve hot or at room temperature with Bread Head from page 188, another crusty loaf, rice, or even over pasta.

When You Need a Vacation from *Timpano*

Bodie's chicken cacciatore

In her old age, our dog Bodie has decided that she only has to eat what she likes to eat. And she has some very particular tastes. A fine steak, *absolutely*. Ground beef, *never*. Scrambled eggs? *Only if smothered with smoked cheddar.*

With such eating habits, keeping her at a healthy weight was a huge challenge. I say "was" and you think I'm going to tell a sob story about how she recently left this mortal coil. But, you'd be wrong. I say "was" because she recently discovered chicken cacciatore.

How did she discover it? Funny story—I'm writing a book which is causing me to cook a lot. And she mostly ignores me. Except on this one dish. Which I now get to cook weekly because it is the only thing that she'll reliably eat. And so I present to you, the best dog food you'll ever have. From my kitchen to yours: Bodie's chicken cacciatore.

—Greg

TOTAL TIME: 1½ hours | **VESSEL:** 4–5 qt Dutch oven | **SERVES:** 4–6

- 1 whole chicken, cut into pieces
- 2 tsp salt, divided
- ¼ tsp pepper
- 1 Tbsp extra-virgin olive oil
- 1 onion, diced
- 6 cloves garlic, minced
- 1 green bell pepper, sliced into ¼-inch strips
- 1 red bell pepper, sliced into ¼-inch strips
- 1 carrot, peeled, diced
- 2 Tbsp tomato paste
- 1 cup red wine
- 1 (28-oz) can pureed tomatoes
- ½ cup black olives, pitted
- ½ tsp dried thyme
- 1 tsp dried basil
- 1 tsp dried oregano
- ½ tsp red pepper flakes (optional)
- 2 Tbsp fresh parsley, chopped

Preheat oven to 375°F. Rub the chicken with 1 teaspoon of salt and pepper.

Add olive oil to a Dutch oven over medium-high heat until the oil shimmers, about 1 minute. Place the chicken in the pot, skin-side down, and let it fry for 3 to 4 minutes, until golden brown.

Turn the chicken, and continue to brown all sides, about 6 to 8 minutes, total. Remove the chicken from the pot and set aside.

Add the onion, garlic, peppers, and carrot to the pot and sauté until they begin to soften, about 7 to 8 minutes. Make a space in the center and add the tomato paste. Fry the paste until fragrant, about 1 minute. Stir in red wine, pureed tomatoes, remaining 1 teaspoon of salt, olives, thyme, basil, oregano, and red pepper flakes, if using, scraping the bottom of the Dutch oven to get any brown bits mixed in. Finally, add the chicken back to the pot, bring to a light simmer, cover, and place in the oven for 45 minutes.

Remove the lid and continue to cook for another 20 to 30 minutes, until the sauce has thickened into a nice gravy.

Garnish with the chopped parsley and serve with rice or potatoes. Feeding the dog is optional.

Peas in the Middle East

A Persian take on an English classic

The ancient Silk Road had a large impact on food from beginning to end, from the Western stretches of Arabia to the center of China. Sitting happily in the middle of the caravan pathway was Persia. The lands around modern-day Iran have been a nexus for intercultural cuisine trade for centuries. Persian cooks have offered as much wisdom as they have absorbed from oases across this storied trade route. Examples abound, where the Chinese have Persians to thank for flatbread, the Persians have the Indians to thank for spice, the Indians and the Persians have the Lebanese to thank for the chickpea.

What if I told you that classic English peas wouldn't be possible without the Silk Road either? During the same time period that the Silk Road was getting pretty busy, a maritime "silk road" was also active. Several varieties of peas native to Greece made their way on these routes to Sicily and from there across to Western Europe. Clearly they were a hit upon becoming a favorite English garden plant and the rest there is history. But, the peas also made their way back down the land route as far as India. Peas are actually quite popular in Iran, as in India. This recipe is an ode to doing something *different* with peas. Finally.

—Howie

TOTAL TIME: 1 hour, 15 minutes | **VESSEL:** 4–5 qt Dutch oven | **SERVES:** 6–8

4 Tbsp extra-virgin olive oil
1 large onion, diced
2 cloves garlic, minced
1 tsp kosher salt
½ tsp ground black pepper
2 tsp ground cumin
1 tsp ground cardamom
½ tsp ground cinnamon
1 lb English peas or edamame (green soybeans), shelled
2 (15-oz) cans chickpeas, with their juices
2 cups vegetable broth
½ lemon

Heat oil in a Dutch oven over medium heat. When the oil begins to shimmer, add onion and sauté, stirring occasionally, for 8 to 10 minutes, or until the onion has begun to caramelize.

Stir in garlic and spices and continue to sauté for 1 minute, until very fragrant. Add peas or edamame, chickpeas, and broth, and increase the heat to medium-high. Bring the mixture to a boil, then reduce the heat to low. Simmer for 20 to 25 minutes, stirring occasionally, or until the mixture is creamy.

Garnish with a squeeze of lemon juice and serve with Persian flatbread, rice, or as a vegetable side to any meal.

One Tipsy Rooster

Yes, you can make coq au vin at home

To me, there is something intimidating about coq au vin. Maybe the deep culinary history of France? Maybe the fear that I'll choose the wrong wine? Maybe the fact that every time I try to say it, my French-speaking partner hits me and tells me that I'm saying it wrong?

Whatever the reason, the intimidation is completely silly. Coq au vin is simple. Chicken. Bacon. Wine. But I would propose that you lean into the intimidation. Use this to impress your next dinner party guests. A menu of *consommé,* coq au vin, and *pots de crème* sounds amazing. Especially when compared to a menu of *broth, chicken stew,* and *pudding,* which sounds like dinner at San Quentin. But we all know the truth: They're the same meal. *Hey! She just hit me again.*

—Greg

TOTAL TIME: 2 hours | **VESSEL:** 6 qt Dutch oven | **SERVES:** 5–6

- 6 chicken thighs, bone-in, skin-on
- ½ tsp salt
- ¼ tsp ground black pepper
- 6 slices bacon
- ½ onion, chopped
- 6–8 mushrooms, sliced
- 2 tsp all-purpose flour
- 1 cup water
- 1½ cups red wine
- 1 tsp dried thyme
- 8–10 pearl onions, peeled and cleaned

Preheat the oven to 400°F.

Season the chicken thighs with the salt and pepper.

Lay the bacon across the bottom of a Dutch oven, and place it in the oven, uncovered, for 15–20 minutes. When the bacon is cooked, but not crispy, remove and set the bacon aside, leaving the bacon fat in the pot.

Place the pot over medium-high heat, and, in two batches, brown the chicken thighs, about 3 to 5 minutes per side. Remove and reserve the chicken, keeping the pot on the heat. Add the onion and mushrooms and sauté for 5 to 7 minutes, or until they begin to brown. Stir the flour into the vegetables and sauté for an additional minute. Pour in the water and wine, using a wooden spoon to scrape up any brown bits. Bring it to a boil and reduce the heat to a light simmer.

Add the thyme and the pearl onions. Chop the bacon into bite-size bits, and add to the pot. Finally, place the chicken back in the pot. The liquid should reach to almost cover the chicken, leaving the skin in the air so that it can remain crispy. (If there is too much liquid, let it boil down a bit. Or, if it is too low, add a bit of water.)

Place the Dutch oven, uncovered, in the oven for 45 minutes, or until the chicken is fully cooked through. Serve hot with crusty bread and other French stuff.

Not-Fake-Pasta Zucchini and Tomatoes

Throw out that spiralizer and actually enjoy this dish

It has recently become popular to thinly cut a zucchini, call it a "noodle" and try to serve it as spaghetti. Which fools exactly nobody. You can't cut the legs off a pair of jeans and call it a swimsuit. Shape does not equal function.

By braising the zucchini in tomato sauce, you actually celebrate, rather than hide, the silky, juicy texture of the summer squash. And with a few minutes of heat, the acid of the tomato has time to get inside the zucchini, accentuating its innate sweetness. A healthy dose of oregano to prevent the tomato taste from being overwhelming, and you've got a bite of summer distilled in your pot.

But I'm not the genius who thought of this. The Greeks have been braising vegetables in tomato sauce for centuries. And the Greeks are no dummies. Just ask Aristotle . . . or Zorba!

—Greg

TOTAL TIME: 30 minutes | **VESSEL:** 3 qt Dutch oven | **SERVES:** 6–8

- 2 Tbsp olive oil
- 1 onion, diced
- 4 cloves garlic, roughly chopped
- 1 Tbsp tomato paste
- 4 medium zucchini, sliced into ½-inch rounds
- 1 (14-oz) can diced tomatoes
- ½ cup water
- ½ tsp oregano
- 1 tsp salt

Add oil to a Dutch oven over medium-high heat. When the oil begins to shimmer, add the onion and sauté for 4 to 5 minutes, until it is soft and a bit clear. Add the garlic and continue to sauté for 30 seconds, until fragrant. Add the tomato paste and stir into the onion, frying for another minute or so.

Add the zucchini, tomatoes (with juice), water, oregano, and salt. Bring to a boil and lower the heat to a light simmer. Allow to simmer, uncovered, for about 20 minutes, until the zucchini is just tender. Serve hot with crusty bread.

Chapter 3
SOUPS

1000 ml
800 ml
600 ml
400 ml
200 ml

All the Bones Broth

Gwyneth would be so proud

To me, bone broth has seemed a bit bizarre as a health-food craze. I mean, I get it, the incredible combination of nutrients and alchemy are good for your bones, joints, digestion, sleep, wound-healing, marriage, superpowers, etc. But, what throws me for a loop is that it took off all of a sudden, while it's basically meat stock that somebody forgot to take off the heat. It *had* to have been an accident, right? I'll accept it as one of the healthier things to come out of a kitchen way behind schedule, but I'll also suggest that it's the way that any stock should be made from here to eternity.

Throughout this book, you'll find that we call for this broth in a great many recipes. The depth of flavor is stunning. The first time you make it and cool it down, you'll chuckle at the texture. It essentially turns into a meaty jello. A more typical stock only cooks for a few hours and has nary a chance to suck all of the collagen from the bones. This stock is cooked so irresponsibly long that gets it *all*. So, don't be put off by the jiggle, bring it to temp and it will all feel *normal* again. I say this in hopes of All the Bones Broth becoming your new normal and you'll be sad that other stocks you meet don't undulate at all.

—Greg

TOTAL TIME: 8–12 hours | **VESSEL:** 7+ qt Dutch oven | **SERVES:** 12–16

- 2 gallons water, divided
- 2 lb beef soup bones or short rib bones
- 1 lb smoked ham hock
- 1 lb chicken bones or carcass from a roasted chicken
- 2 heads garlic, halved widthwise
- 3 leeks, trimmed, halved, washed
- 1 small hand ginger, halved lengthwise
- 2 Tbsp rice vinegar

Preheat the oven to 400°F.

In a large pot, bring 1 gallon of water to a boil and add bones in batches if necessary, each for 5 minutes. Remove and rinse the bones. Discard the water. Place bones on a sheet pan and transfer to the oven and roast for 15 minutes. Remove the bones from the oven.

Add all bones and the remaining ingredients, including 1 gallon of water to a Dutch oven over medium-high heat. Bring the mixture to a boil. Reduce the heat to low, cover the pot with a lid and allow it to simmer for at least 8 hours, ideally 12 hours.

Uncover the pot, remove the bones and any large debris. Strain the broth through a (very) fine-meshed sieve, cheesecloth, or a straining bag. The finer the strain, the cleaner the broth. Add some salt and sip on a delicious mug of broth; use it for soups like the *One-*Pot Ramen on page 97 or for Yes, Grandma, We'll Call It Gravy on page 19.

Pasta Fazool!

Or at least that's what I thought it was called

What kid can make the jump from *bizgott* to biscotti? *Galamad* to calamari? *Ganol* to cannoli? *Mutzadell* to mozzarella? I guess it's the same kid who understands that Italian Americans and Italians sound almost entirely different. The same kid that knows that *pasta fazool* means macaroni and beans, and knows what *fagioli* is. That kid wasn't me. I came up surrounded by words and cultural gems that I figured must be *just like Italy*. Now that I think about it, Dean Martin didn't help matters. When he sang of *pasta fazool*, I thought, *finally, outside confirmation! That's Amoré, That's Italian!*

Language quirks aside, I did discover early on that pasta and beans was delicious, no matter what anyone anywhere called it. Creamy beans, sumptuous macaroni with a little bit of a bite, unctuous meat, punchy tomato, and a topping of earthy Parmesan cheese. This was a dish I could eat a lot and we all need to eat more, though it seems fairly old-school, no? If you read back to my story from the Yes, Grandma, We'll Call It Gravy recipe from page 19, you'll note that most Sundays in Union City offered pasta and gravy—which I adore. But, every once in a while, pasta fazool would be on the stove when we arrived and made my day. Let it make yours.

—Howie

TOTAL TIME: 40 minutes | **VESSEL:** 3–5 qt Dutch oven | **SERVES:** 6–8

- 2 Tbsp extra-virgin olive oil
- 4 oz Italian sausage, casings removed (optional)
- 1 large onion, diced
- 4 ribs celery, diced
- 5 cloves garlic, minced
- 1 tsp salt
- ½ tsp ground black pepper
- 2 (15-oz) cans white beans, with their liquid
- 2 cups Yes, Grandma, We'll Call It Gravy from page 19, or other tomato sauce
- 6 cups vegetable or chicken stock
- 1 cup dry ditalini or orzo pasta
- Chopped parsley and grated Parmesan cheese, for garnish

Add oil to a Dutch oven over medium-high heat. Add sausage and sauté until browned, about 4 to 5 minutes, breaking it up as it cooks. Add onion and celery and continue to sauté until softened, about 6 to 8 minutes. Add garlic, salt, and pepper and continue to sauté for 1 minute.

Add beans, their liquid, gravy or tomato sauce, and stock, and bring it to a boil. Reduce the heat, add the pasta, put a lid on the pot, and simmer until the pasta is cooked, about 8 to 10 minutes.

Remove the lid and ladle hot scoops into anxiously waiting bowls, garnish with parsley and Parmesan, and enjoy!

One-Pot Ramen

A complicated Japanese soup, simplified

Often, it's the low-profile, hardly visible eateries that change your perspective the most. Some years back on a visit to Tokyo, after a chilly and muddy morning of hiking in the seaside suburb of Kamakura, I stepped into a dream. A crude depiction of a steaming noodle bowl on a modest storefront window seemed downright comforting. I ducked through a thin curtain separating the busy street from a delicious steam cloud.

This joint was a small, savory sauna, a temple of soup. It furnished seats for a slender eight, but somehow it wasn't cramped. The wife and husband team of purveyors were the only staff, this cute and artful kitchen was an extension of their home. As the rooster crows, she's deep into making hand-pulled noodles, as he crafts an expert broth from the bones of chicken, pork and beef, seaweed, and dried tuna flakes.

They wittily finish my order of the popular "Buddha Bowl" with two "eyebrows" of scallions, two "eyes" of boiled egg, a "nose" of tempura crab leg and a red pepper grin. To the last slurp, the noodles had a pleasant toothiness, a smooth yet satisfying game for the teeth, but it was the broth that was the lingering star of the show. Flavorful but not fishy, punchy but not salty, full-bodied but not thick. It's complex and typical of really good ramen shops across Japan. Your life can be simpler. Enjoy shortcut ramen on us!

—Howie

TOTAL TIME: Time from sub-recipes, plus 30 minutes | **VESSEL:** 3–5 qt Dutch oven | **SERVES:** 3–4

8 cups All the Bones Broth from page 93, or chicken or beef stock
2/3 cup light soy sauce
1 tsp kosher salt
8 oz baby spinach
10 oz dry ramen noodles
4–6 eggs, poached
8–10 slices of Adobo Entendre from page 29, cooked pork belly, or other cooked meat of choice
1 carrot, shredded
6 scallions, thinly sliced

In a Dutch oven over medium-high heat, bring the stock and soy sauce to a boil. Reduce heat to medium and maintain a high simmer. Add salt and spinach to the broth and cook until the spinach completely wilts. Add noodles and allow them to cook for 4 minutes, stirring occasionally so they do not stick together. Turn off the heat.

Dress the top of the ramen with poached eggs, sliced meat, carrot shreds, and scallions. Have folks take servings of combinations at will.

The Easiest Chicken Soup in the World

We're not kidding

During one of our relatively misguided trips to China, Howie and I toured around the east coast during a cold and rainy February. We happened upon Xishan, which is a resort island outside of Suzhou. This being winter, the whole island was basically shut down for business. Wet. Bone-chilling. Desolate. But, we were naturally hungry and forged ahead to the best place to find out where they keep their food, the morning farm market!

We asked a local resident about the best place to eat that wasn't boarded up for the season. She gave us a name "Little Fish," and vague walking directions through a series of alleyways that lead to nothing that looked like a restaurant. No signs, we just kept calling out, "Little Fish, Little Fish, does anyone know Little Fish?" Eventually, and likely as a result of our disrupting the neighborhood, someone led us by the hand to Little Fish and what still didn't look like a restaurant. The central courtyard looked like the playground of a preschool. Turns out it looked that way because it was. But, through the courtyard there was a kitchen, and beside the kitchen was a 3-table dining room. Talk about hidden gems.

Upon seeing our frozen, soaked, lumbering selves show up for something to warm the soul, Little Fish showed us what China was made of and sat us down for a meal. Actually, a single soup. Out came a huge ceramic bowl filled with what became the way we define chicken soup. It was gorgeous in its simplicity: chicken, water, scallions, and salt. Most impressively, it was the most chicken-y chicken we've tasted. Part of the challenge that we have in re-creating this soup at home, is that we typically get our chickens from the supermarket, not from the courtyard. Did I forget to mention that there were eight chickens pecking around that preschool playground? Or was it seven?

—Greg

TOTAL TIME: 6 hours | **VESSEL:** 4½+ qt Dutch oven | **SERVES:** 6–8

4–5 lb whole chicken
½ bunch scallions, halved
3 Tbsp kosher salt
Water to barely cover

Place all ingredients in a Dutch oven over medium-low heat and bring to a simmer. Reduce the heat to the lowest heat place a lid on the pot. Allow the chicken to barely simmer for 6 hours.

Remove the lid. At this point, the chicken should be falling apart. Optionally, use a slotted spoon to remove the chicken pieces, allow them to cool, and pick off the meat. Again, optionally, strain the broth of debris and serve in a large soup terrine with the picked chicken.

If you opt out of the cleansing suggestions above, bring the pot to the table and give everyone a bowl. Have them take some soup and some chicken and get all medieval on it. Best. Easiest. Soup. Ever.

If Clouds Tasted Like Tubers

A potato leek soup to dream about

One does not often associate *light and airy* with potato leek soup. It's more frequently part of the conversation around soul-satisfying or comfort foods. *That'll fill your belly good!* Heck, even the name potato leek soup *sounds* heavy, doesn't it? Nothing refreshing about it. That is, until you try this recipe on for size. The combination of a healthy dose of comparatively crisp vegetables and the blending process, the potato may seem to play second fiddle in the final texture, but certainly doesn't get the shaft.

The first time I devised the idea of reimagining potato leek soup, I was serving it at the start of multi-course meal for many guests. When I shared my idea with my wife, she thought I was nuts. *You can't serve this soup and expect people to keep eating. It's crazy.* Well, I've been the crazy one before. One spoonful into the soup, my wife and skeptical guests gave a collective sigh of relief. We cleaned the pot and continued with 4 more courses. Reading is not believing, and this is pretty unbelievable. Cook. Your dinner guests will be amazed.

—Howie

TOTAL TIME: 1 hour | **VESSEL:** 5–6 qt Dutch Oven | **SERVES:** 4–6

- 10 cups chicken or vegetable stock
- 3 lb russet or Yukon Gold potatoes, peeled, cut into 2-inch pieces
- 4 leeks, trimmed, halved lengthwise, washed, thinly sliced
- 4 ribs celery, diced
- 1 Tbsp salt
- 2 tsp ground black pepper
- 5 sprigs fresh oregano
- ⅔ cup heavy cream
- ½ bunch chives, thinly sliced

Place stock, potatoes, leeks, celery, salt, pepper, and oregano sprigs in a Dutch oven and heat on medium-high. When the stock begins to boil, reduce the heat to medium-low and simmer for 15 to 20 minutes, or until the potatoes can be easily pierced with a knife.

Carefully transfer the contents of the pot to a very large heat-resistant mixing bowl and remove the sprigs of oregano. Puree either with an immersion blender or in several batches in a standing blender. Transfer puree back to the pot over medium heat, stir in the cream, and continue to cook for 10 minutes. Remove from the heat.

Ladle into bowls, garnish with chives, and serve alone or with bread or croutons.

Boris's Mom's Borscht

Beets save lives!

Some years back I was doing a week-long teaching gig in Kyrgyzstan. I spent my off time hanging out with my local contact, Boris. Great guy. One day during our lunch break, we headed to the cafeteria at the American University of Kyrgyzstan. I was totally curious as to what was on offer. As my luck would have it, the food was horrible and to top it all off, gunshots rang just outside the window next to which I was choking down a terrible rendition of a cheeseburger. Frankly, I couldn't decide which was worse, but the gunfight gave me a great excuse to get far away from that food!

The shooting turned out to be the beginning of a rebellious mob on their way to storm the presidential palace—at which they succeeded some hours later. Boris, fearing for his reputation as a good host whose guests don't normally die, offered to quickly drive me a few hours away to his family's home on the bullet-free shores of Lake Issykkul! His family was a pleasant alternative to heavily armed revolutionaries. Boris's parents were both Russian born but moved to Kyrgyzstan when Boris was young. He grew up on his mother's borscht and fish-head soup, both of which were already at the table upon our arrival, and one of which I could actually eat. The borscht was fantastic enough to want to replicate at home. Forever, it will be the taste of getting out of Kyrgyzstan without any extra holes.

—Howie

TOTAL TIME: 1 hour | **VESSEL:** 3–5 qt Dutch oven | **SERVES:** 6–8

- 2–3 medium beets, peeled, shredded
- 1 small red onion, shredded
- 1 medium carrot, shredded
- 1 tsp kosher salt
- ½ tsp ground black pepper
- 7 cups All the Bones Broth from page 93, or beef stock
- ½ small head green cabbage, shredded
- 2 Tbsp butter
- Sour cream and dill, for garnish

In a Dutch oven over medium-high heat, add beets, onion, carrot, salt, pepper, and broth or stock. Bring the mixture to a boil, then reduce the heat to low and simmer for 25 minutes.

Stir in cabbage and butter and continue to simmer for 25 minutes.

Serve hot with a dollop of sour cream and pulled fronds of dill.

Italian Weddings Must Get Messy

But this soup is delicious

Everyone has their feelings about cafeteria food. To me, my college cafeteria was always a place for food experimentation. I would make healthy use of the salad bar, the waffle station, the deli bins, and poach raw ingredients to create something new that I actually wanted to eat. Where the steam-table dishes from the cafeteria generally weren't terrific, there were a few things that stood out and were frankly made pretty well. Their Italian wedding soup was *good*. It also felt like I was eating something cultural. *Ooh, they must serve this at weddings.* Every bowl felt like a celebration.

Then, I found out that it had *nothing* to do with weddings. It's not even particularly poetic. The greens don't represent the bride. The meatballs don't stand for the groom. The pasta isn't an allusion to the family and friends in attendance. Dang it! That would have been awesome. The name comes from the fact that within this soup vegetables are paired with meat. That's it. Boring, right? Well, good thing for Italian wedding soup that the dish itself is fabulous and the combination of beef, spinach, and orzo is like magic.

—Greg

TOTAL TIME: 55 minutes | **VESSEL:** 4½–6 qt Dutch oven | **SERVES:** 6–8

- ½ recipe meatballs from Yes, Grandma, We'll Call It Gravy from page 19, uncooked
- 2 Tbsp extra-virgin olive oil
- 2 leeks, trimmed, halved lengthwise, washed, diced
- ½ bunch celery, diced
- 2 carrots, diced
- 1 tsp kosher salt
- 4 cloves garlic, minced
- ½ cup dry white wine
- 6 cups beef or chicken stock
- ½ bunch parsley, roughly chopped
- 6 oz baby spinach, roughly chopped
- 8 oz orzo or other small pasta
- Parmesan cheese, grated, for garnish

Preheat the oven to 400°F.

Form the meatballs smaller than normal, as this is a soup. Place the balls on a sheet pan and roast in the oven for 12 minutes while you start the remainder of the soup. Remember to remove them from the oven at the appropriate time and set aside.

Add olive oil to a Dutch oven over medium heat. Add leeks, celery, carrots, and salt and sauté until the vegetables soften but do not brown, about 6 to 8 minutes. Add garlic and continue to sauté for 2 minutes. Add wine and allow it to reduce for 4 minutes.

Add stock, increase the heat to medium-high, and bring to a boil. Reduce the heat to low and add parsley and spinach. Stir to ensure the spinach wilts completely. Transfer the meatballs into the soup. Place the lid on the pot and allow it to simmer for 10 minutes.

Remove the lid from the pot and stir in pasta. Replace the lid and continue to simmer until the pasta is cooked, about 15 minutes.

Remove the lid and serve hot, beautiful ladles full of wedding bliss. Well, you know what we mean. Garnish with Parmesan for a deliciously salty umami bite.

Soup Shan't Be Boring

Making magic with pasta and broccoli

Soup can be a drag. But, what if it were green? Green is always fun! Think about it: recycling is green, US cash is green, meadows are green, mint chocolate chip is green. I'll tell you what's green but not always fun: broccoli and spinach. How do we get them onto that list of fun? Put them in a big pot with onions, garlic, basil, and cream, and blend them! Party time!

—Greg

TOTAL TIME: 50 minutes | **VESSEL:** 4–6 qt Dutch oven | **SERVES:** 8–10

- 4 Tbsp extra-virgin olive oil, divided
- 1 large onion, diced
- 4 cloves garlic, roughly chopped
- 6 cups All the Bones Broth from page 93, or vegetable or chicken stock
- 1 lb broccoli, large florets, stems diced
- 2 tsp kosher salt
- ½ tsp ground black pepper
- 10 oz baby spinach
- 6 basil leaves 1 cup cream
- 1 recipe The Pot Lid Can Do That? biscuit dough from page 208, uncooked (optional)
- 8 oz ditalini, orzo, or other small pasta

Preheat the oven to 400°F.

Heat oil in a Dutch oven over medium heat. When the oil begins to shimmer, add onion and sauté, stirring occasionally, for 6 to 8 minutes, or until the onion has softened but not browned. Add the garlic and continue to sauté for 1 minute. Add broth or stock and bring to a simmer over medium-high heat.

Add broccoli, salt, and pepper, and simmer for 5 minutes. Add spinach and basil and simmer for an additional 3 minutes. Puree either with an immersion blender or in several batches in a standing blender. Transfer Puree back to the pot over medium heat, stir in the cream, and remove from the heat.

If including the lid biscuits: Grease the underside of the Dutch oven lid with 1 tablespoon of olive oil. Cut out dough rounds with a 3-inch biscuit cutter or the top of a 3-inch-wide glass. Place the dough rounds on top of the flipped lid, butting up against each other to fit as many as possible. And place the remainder on a greased sheet pan. Drizzle 2 remaining tablespoons of olive oil over the biscuit dough.

Stir in the pasta and transfer the otherwise filled Dutch oven with the lid on upside down to the oven and bake until biscuits are starting to brown, about 20 to 25 minutes. Remove the pot from the oven and serve the biscuits with delicious soup.

Your Date Should *Also* Have Sopa de Ajo

One seriously garlicky Spanish garlic soup

If you've read Greg's treatise on Vampire-Proof Meatballs from page 3, you have a handle on how much garlic is too much garlic for any mere mortal, and if you've cooked his meatballs, you've already gone beyond such a limit. Hope you liked them as much as I do. But here, we offer yet another, dare I say, much more pure garlic bomb in a humble soup. The best part, it's loaded with bread which soaks up all of that evil/genius goop. So, better to have everyone around the table enjoy a steamy bowl so you can actually converse afterward.

I first met Spanish garlic soup upon moving to Barcelona, and my wife and I sat for a fixed-price lunch. The deal was always the same at a place around the block from my apartment, €10 for a soup, a tapa, and a dessert. She chose a cold melon soup—I'll never understand cold soup, who wants to sip their salad? I opted for the garlic soup. I simply didn't understand how difficult it would be to be around me after lunch. And so began my love affair with both Spanish cooking and breath mints.

—Howie

TOTAL TIME: 20 minutes | **VESSEL:** 5–6 qt Dutch oven | **SERVES:** 6–8

- ⅔ cup extra-virgin olive oil
- 20 cloves garlic, minced
- 2½ Tbsp smoked paprika
- 1 tsp onion powder
- 2 tsp kosher salt
- 1 lb ciabatta or other crusty bread, diced
- 1½ cup dry white wine
- 10 cups vegetable broth
- 5 eggs, beaten
- 1 bunch parsley, roughly chopped, for garnish

In a Dutch oven over medium heat, add the olive oil. When the oil begins to shimmer after about 2 minutes, add the garlic, paprika, onion powder, and salt. Sauté until the garlic begins to brown slightly, about 1½ minutes. Add the bread and continue to sauté until the bread begins to toast, about 4 to 5 minutes.

Pour the wine into the skillet, increase the heat to medium-high, and allow the wine to reduce and get completely absorbed by the bread, about 3 minutes. Pour in broth and allow the mixture to come to a visible simmer. Stirring in a constant circular motion, slowly drizzle in the beaten eggs. They should cook within about 1 minute.

Serve the soup hot with a garnish of parsley.

Avgolemono

Almost as fun to say as "osso buco"

Avgolemono is my favorite soup. So simple. So creamy. So amazing. It is, in some cases, a bit too good. I have a friend—we'll keep her name out of it. Out of a love for animals, she decided to become a vegetarian. And she kept to that pledge for more than ten years. Over that time, we regularly ate Greek food. And when I eat Greek, I eat Avgolemono.

For ten years, she watched me order. Saw me quiver with anticipation, smile with the bowl's delivery, and savor every last spoonful. Until finally, she couldn't take it. The woman who resisted bacon and hamburgers, steak and shrimp—she just had to try avgolemono. With that one bite, she was hooked.

Some people hide their doll collection. Others hide their gambling. For her, the secret shame was her obsession with avgolemono. So, enjoy this recipe. But beware, avgolemono is highly addictive.

—Greg

TOTAL TIME: 30 minutes | **VESSEL:** 3 qt Dutch oven | **SERVES:** 4–6

6 cups chicken broth
1 tsp kosher salt
¾ cup white rice, uncooked
4 eggs
Juice of 4 lemons (about ¾ cup)
¼ cup parsley, chopped

Add broth to a Dutch oven over medium-high heat. Bring to a boil and lower the heat to a light simmer. Stir in the salt and rice. Cover, and allow to boil for 15 minutes, or until the rice is fully cooked and beginning to thicken the soup. Turn off the heat.

In a large bowl, whisk the eggs thoroughly. While whisking, slowly pour ½ cup of the soup into the eggs. Continue to whisk and repeat with a second ½ cup. Once it is well combined, pour the whole egg mixture into the Dutch oven with the broth, and whisk until well combined. The soup should be thickened and a bit frothy.

Stir in lemon juice, top with some parsley, and serve hot.

Putting the Butter Back in Butternut Squash Soup

Enough said

I've thought about it, and yeah, I'm fine with the name *butternut*, but I have to protest the word *squash*. You see, the farmer that first crossed breeds of squash to generate the butternut claimed the flesh was silky like *butter*, and had a flavor that evoked a *nut*. That's all well and good. But, *squash* derived from a Native American term meaning to consume something *raw*. Look, I rant about food words being appropriated all the time. Don't get me started on *paella* or *bolognese*! Squash is a special one. It's *literally* wrong, lest you fancy gnawing on uncooked squash. Argh, I can't even get away with not typing the darned word!

One could argue that it would be better to rename all *squash* to be *gourds*. Technically, some but not all squashes are indeed gourds. Yet, isn't it far superior to use a term of something of a sibling rather than confuse people by suggesting chomping on a freshly picked pumpkin? If we stick with the term *squash*, I hereby claim: You can also name your dog "Cat."

—Howie

TOTAL TIME: 1 hour | **VESSEL:** 3–5 qt Dutch oven | **SERVES:** 4–6

2 Tbsp extra-virgin olive oil
¼ cup butter
1 large onion, diced
3 cloves garlic
2 tsp smoked paprika
1 tsp salt
½ tsp ground black pepper
4 cups vegetable or chicken stock
1–1½ lb butternut squash, peeled, seeded, and cut into 1-inch pieces

Add oil and butter to a Dutch oven over medium heat. When the butter melts, add the onion and sauté until it begins to brown at the edges, about 8 to 10 minutes. Add the garlic, paprika, salt, and pepper and continue to sauté for 2 minutes. Add stock and bring to a boil over medium-high heat. Reduce the heat to medium and stir in squash pieces. Allow the squash to simmer, covered, until soft, about 12 to 15 minutes.

Carefully transfer the contents of the pot to a very large heat-resistant mixing bowl. Puree either with an immersion blender or in several batches in a standing blender. Ladle into bowls and slurp happy or serve with Bread Head from page 188, another crusty exemplar.

LODGE
CAST IRON

Cioppino Noir

A rather cynical oceanic stew with a heart of gold

Okay, right out of the gate, *I am the cynical stew.* The subtitle is about me. If it's not clear by now, I have many opinions about food names and origin stories and I am not bashful about letting you know. Words matter and history matters, right? So, it pains me to run into a dish like cioppino which leans heavily upon its heritage as a San Francisco invention but has a solid historical footprint in Italy.

One story goes that an industrious Italian American fisherman came up with the idea for this soup after a long day on the water, and tossed whatever he had left over from the catch into a pot and magic was the result. Another story has a group of fishermen cooking on their boat during a longer-than-normal haul. They used whatever provisions they could add to the seafood they caught to create some sustenance. So, onions, canned tomato, and wine.

Both stories are quaint and would make perfect sense if it weren't for the tiny step from *cioppino* to *ciuppin*, an Italian dialectical word meaning to chop small. *Ciuppin* is also the name of a Genovese seafood stew with similar backstory about fishermen. Go figure. Now, the one saving grace for the American origin tales is that the tomato is a New World vegetable and they were introduced into Italy from the Americas around the time that both soups were made popular. Chicken or the egg?

—Howie

TOTAL TIME: 50 minutes | **VESSEL:** 4½+ qt Dutch oven | **SERVES:** 4–6

- ¼ cup extra-virgin olive oil
- 1 large onion, diced
- 1½ tsp kosher salt
- 5 cloves garlic, roughly chopped
- 4 Tbsp tomato paste
- 1 Tbsp sambal olek or other chile paste (optional)
- 2 cups Pinot Noir or other dry red wine
- 1 (28-oz) can crushed tomatoes
- 2 cups water
- 3 Tbsp soy sauce
- 12 oz mussels, cleaned, beards removed (discard any that are open)
- 12 oz shrimp, peeled, deveined
- 12 oz cod fillets, cut into 2-inch pieces
- 12 oz bay scallops or quartered sea scallops, tough side muscles discarded

Add olive oil to a Dutch oven over medium-high heat. When the oil begins to shimmer, add onion and salt and sauté until translucent, about 8 to 10 minutes. Add garlic and continue to sauté until very fragrant, about 2 to 3 minutes. Stir in tomato paste and chile paste, if using, and sauté for 2 minutes. Stir in wine, bring to a boil, and cook for 4 minutes. Stir in tomatoes, water, and soy sauce, bring to a boil, reduce the heat to low, and simmer for 20 minutes.

Stir in the fish and seafood, cover the pot, and continue to simmer until the mussels have opened and the other proteins have cooked through, about 7 to 9 minutes. Remove the lid and serve immediately with the crustiest of breads for delicious dipping. We recommend ladling some of the broth into a separate bowl, as dipping bread will consume the average diner.

In Hominy with Pozole

That's hilarious; it's also corn stew

The genius of this book is clearly the one-pot cooking of most recipes. This soup, however requires *two* cooking vessels. I know, that's *double* the dishwashing. And a blender and a strainer, which seems like entirely too much work. It also means buying ingredients you probably don't have handy, like whole dried chiles and a can of hominy. So, if I bought this book instead of writing it, I'd probably skip to something else. I'd be making a huge mistake.

Pozole is amazing. Meaty, spicy, sweet, succulent, crunchy, and acidic—all in one bite. And while it seems complicated, it really isn't. You are just boiling stuff in two pots and combining it. So, I strongly recommend giving this one a shot. And if you don't like it, I hereby give you permission to call me a liar.

—Greg

TOTAL TIME: 3–4 hours | **VESSEL:** 6+ qt Dutch oven | **SERVES:** 8–10

FOR THE POZOLE:

3 qt water

6 dried guajillo chiles (New Mexico or California chiles will also do)

1 Tbsp vegetable or canola oil

1½ lb pork shoulder, boneless, large diced

4 cloves garlic, minced

1 (30-oz) can hominy, drained and rinsed

2 bay leaves

½ tsp ground cumin

1 Tbsp dried oregano

4 tsp salt

FOR THE GARNISHES:

1 cup shredded cabbage

2 Tbsp fresh oregano

2 limes, sliced

6 radishes, thinly sliced

1 cup crispy tortillas, broken into bite sizes

1 avocado, sliced

Boil water in a Dutch oven over medium-high heat, then reduce the heat to low and maintain a simmer.

While the water is heating, take off the stems and seeds of your dried chiles. Place a skillet over medium heat. Once the pan is hot, take half the chiles and place them in the dry skillet. Allow them to toast until fragrant, but not burned, about 1½ to 2 minutes. Repeat with the second batch. Place the toasted chiles in a heatproof bowl and pour in 2 cups of the simmering water.

Wipe out the skillet and add oil over medium-high heat. When the oil begins to shimmer, add the pork pieces in batches to not overcrowd the pot. Brown the meat on all sides, 6 to 8 minutes for each batch, then remove the pork directly to the Dutch oven with simmering water.

To the skillet, add garlic and sauté for 30 seconds before pouring in 1 cup of the simmering water. Use a wooden spoon to scrape up the brown bits and then pour the garlic water into Dutch oven of simmering water and pork.

(Directions continued on next page)

To the Dutch oven with simmering water and pork, stir in the hominy, bay leaves, cumin, oregano, and 4 teaspoons of salt.

While the soup is coming back to a boil, pour the chiles and their soaking liquid into a blender. Leave the top of the blender cracked to avoid steam buildup while blending for 1 to 2 minutes, or until completely smooth. Pour the puree through a fine strainer into the Dutch oven. Use the back of a wooden spoon to push as much of the chile liquid as possible through the strainer. Discard the pulp.

Partially cover the Dutch oven and bring to a boil over medium-high heat, then turn the heat down to a light simmer. Allow the soup to cook for 2 to 3 hours, or until you just can't take it anymore.

While the soup is cooking, prepare some or all of the pozole garnishes, keeping each in a separate bowl. Serve piping hot, allowing each person to build their own perfect soup out of the various garnishes.

Chapter 4

CASSEROLES

Oaxacasserole

"Mexican rice" will never be the same

If you read back to our recipe for Those Beans from That Mexican Place from page 52, you'll see that I feel strongly about restaurant beans. They so often get very little attention, though they are frequently the best thing on the plate. Well, I feel the exact opposite about Mexican restaurant rice. It's confusing. There are so many simple ways to make rice delicious that boring rice with one's enchiladas and beans almost seems intentional.

You might jump to the conclusion that every *other* rice culture in the world has it figured out, but Mexico missed out. You'd be mistaken. In this book, we present not one but two *arrozes* from south of the border that will stick in your mind like Smashmouth's "Allstar." When you're enjoying your next molé chicken down the street, you'll glance across the plate and wish you were cooking at home instead. Make this Oaxacan gem or the Arroz Verde from page 153, save a little cash, and make everyone happy. Adios.

—Greg

TOTAL TIME: 1 hour, 30 minutes | **VESSEL:** 4–5 qt Dutch oven | **SERVES:** 4–6

- 3 Tbsp extra-virgin olive oil
- 1 onion, diced
- 3 cloves garlic, roughly chopped
- 2 poblano peppers, roasted, peeled, seeded, diced
- 1 tsp kosher salt
- 2 tsp ground cumin
- 1 tsp ground annato or ground achiote seed (optional)
- 2 tsp ancho or other chile powder
- 4 cups chicken stock
- 1 cup diced green beans
- 1 cup corn kernels
- 2 cups long-grain white rice, uncooked
- 6 oz mozzarella or Monterey Jack cheese, shredded

Preheat the oven to 400°F.

Heat a Dutch oven over medium heat and add the olive oil. When the oil begins to shimmer, add the onion and sauté, stirring often until it begins to caramelize, about 12 to 15 minutes. Add garlic, roasted peppers, and spices and continue to sauté until very fragrant, about 3–4 minutes. Add stock, green beans, and corn, increase the heat to medium-high, and bring to a boil. Reduce the heat to low and simmer for 10 minutes.

Add the rice, cover, and transfer the pot to the oven and braise for 35 minutes. Carefully remove the cover, stir the contents evenly, distribute cheese across the top, and continue to cook uncovered for 10 minutes. Remove the pot from the oven. Allow the rice to rest for 15 minutes. Serve directly to bowls, including some cheese with every serving.

You'll Flip for this Lebanese Eggplant Rice

No, seriously, you have to flip the pot!

I have walked a good amount of this earth in search of culinary inspiration. If you read the narrative segments of our other books, you'd jump to the conclusion that we're Asia-focused with the occasional nod to Europe. But, perhaps unexpectedly, a good amount of my culinary ethic comes straight out of the Middle East. Indeed, some of the best meals of my life were served in Jordan! By the way, I know I'll get in trouble for saying this, but all the great food from the region should be called what it is: *Lebanese*. After all, the Levant is the spiritual homeland of Middle Eastern cuisine. I'm ready for your scorn.

On my first trip to Amman, I spent my first day strolling the desert in search of myself and some good Greco-Roman ruins. The Middle East is awesome for spotting seemingly random temples in the middle of nowhere, with nary a tourist in sight. Anyhow, once I found myself and left some truly cool ancient columns in the dust, I was hungry. As randomly as I bumped into ruins, I luckily bumped into a roadside café with a terrace overlooking the vast sands. Perfect! The menu had all the small-plate hits I had looked forward to trying, and then some.

As is my norm, I asked the server to suggest something that I hadn't thought of. After a few questions, and then a glass of ice-cold beer, he brought out *maqlubah*. Layers of creamy eggplant, peppers, olives, and highly seasoned rice. It took me by complete surprise, and I've been studying the dish for a couple of decades in order to come up with what you see below. And yes, at the very end you will flip the casserole out of the Dutch oven, so start working out now.

—Howie

TOTAL TIME: 2 hours | **VESSEL:** 2 (1½ qt) Dutch ovens or, if you're brave, 1 (3 qt) Dutch oven | **SERVES:** 6–8

2 Tbsp extra-virgin olive oil, plus 2 cups, divided
1 large onion, diced
1½ tsp kosher salt
½ tsp ground black pepper
4 cloves garlic, roughly chopped
1 medium tomato, halved, grated, skins discarded
2 tsp ground cumin
3 tsp ground turmeric
1 tsp za'atar herb mix or dried thyme
¼ tsp ground cinnamon
4 cups water, plus more to soak rice
2 cups basmati or other long-grain rice, uncooked
2 large Italian eggplants, ½-inch-wide lengthwise slices
8 oz pitted olives, halved
2 roasted red peppers, thinly sliced
4 oz toasted pine nuts

Add 2 tablespoons olive oil to a pot over medium-high heat. Add onion, 1 teaspoon salt, and pepper, and sauté for 6–8 minutes or until the onion begins to brown. Add garlic, tomato, cumin, and turmeric and continue to sauté for 3 minutes, or until the

(Directions continued on next page)

liquid from the tomato has evaporated. Add za'atar, cinnamon, and 4 cups of water and bring to a boil. Reduce the heat to low and allow the mixture to simmer for 30 minutes.

While the seasoned liquid is simmering, in a mixing bowl, cover the rice with water by one inch and set aside.

In a separate skillet, add ¼ cup of olive oil over medium heat. When the oil begins to shimmer, add eggplant slices in batches, sprinkle with a pinch of salt, and fry on each side for 1½ minutes. As the eggplant is cooked, transfer to a paper towel–lined plate.

Preheat the oven to 375°F.

Remove the simmering stock from the heat. Strain the onion mixture over a bowl to retain the stock. Drain the soaking rice.

In a 3-quart Dutch oven or two 1½-quart Dutch ovens, begin to construct the layers. If using two smaller pots, simply evenly distribute the ingredients. Begin by placing overlapping long slices of cooked eggplant at the bottom of the pot, starting at the center draping up the sides. Then, scatter olives and ½ of the red peppers, then ½ of the pine nuts, followed by a layer of the onion mixture. Evenly distribute drained rice across the top, obscuring the other ingredients. Carefully pour the stock over the rice, trying not to disturb its placement atop the rest of the pot. Place a lid on the pot(s) and transfer to the oven to roast for 45 minutes.

Remove the pot(s) from the oven and allow them to rest for 10 minutes. Remove the lid(s) and place a plate large enough to fit the Dutch oven, or a flat board over the top of the pot. With a firm grip on both the plate/board and the pot handles, carefully flip the pot so that the plate/board sits below. Place the duo down on a work surface and allow them to sit together for an additional 10 minutes.

Tap the bottom and sides of the pot(s) with a wooden spoon several times. Gently lift the pot(s) away from the *maqlubah*. Good luck. After the crowd stops applauding, serve hot scoops garnished with remaining peppers and pine nuts as a one-pot meal.

Hong Kong in a Pot

The yin and yang of tofu and mushrooms

The schools of Chinese gastronomy, according to tradition, and most generically lie in the four corners of the country. In the North, food is salty, in the East, food is sweet, in the West, food is spicy, and in the South, food is delicate. The word "delicate" has always struck me as a strange way of describing food. I suppose, when you consider South China favorites like dim sum, there are a great many dumpling formats that are intricately crafted. But delicate? Nevertheless, the style of cooking that always reminds me of Guangdong and Hong Kong is clay pot cooking, which is the opposite of delicate!

While traveling in the South, the street stalls that would stop me in my tracks had rows of little propane burners topped with earthen casseroles with lids that hid secrets as yet to be revealed. When those lids lifted, through billows of steam, my meal began to take shape. Would it be smothered seafood over noodles? Perhaps red-cooked pork shoulder with potatoes? Maybe that Hong Kong celebrity, braised sausage and chicken over rice? The last has always been my delicious default.

When cooking at home, I've enthusiastically replicated the tastes and experiences of the Chinese street. But, as I've aged and have begun leaning closer to a plant-based diet, I've started to investigate how vegetables are treated in Chinese kitchens. I've never felt something was missing when enjoying purely vegetarian dishes at even hole-in-the-wall places across China. This dish explores both the non-delicate cookery of Hong Kong and treats vegetables in such a way that satisfies the belly *and* the soul. The method below serves up a meaty layer of tofu, mushrooms, and greens, hovering above a bed of rice that both retains its own identity yet is steeped through with saucy drippings from the veggies above. This is next-level vegetarian.

—Howie

TOTAL TIME: 1 hour, 55 minutes | **VESSEL:** 1.5 qt Dutch oven | **SERVES:** 1–2

1 cup jasmine or other long-grain rice, uncooked
1¼ cup water, divided, plus more for rinsing
¼ cup canola or vegetable oil
10 oz cremini or shiitake mushrooms, stems discarded, sliced thinly
½ tsp kosher salt
4 cloves garlic, minced
½ inch ginger, peeled, minced
4 scallions, thinly sliced, white and green parts separated
3 Tbsp light soy sauce
3 Tbsp dark soy sauce
4 Tbsp oyster-flavored sauce (vegetarian)
⅛ tsp liquid smoke (optional)
¼ tsp MSG (optional)
4 oz smoked or baked tofu, thinly sliced
4 oz chard leaves, thinly sliced

In a mixing bowl, rinse the rice until the water runs nearly clear, about 3 to 4 times. Place drained rice and 1 cup of fresh water in a Dutch oven, off the heat. Cover and set aside for 1 hour.

(Directions continued on page 127)

Preheat the oven to 350°F.

30 minutes into the rice soaking, add oil to a skillet over medium-high heat. Add mushrooms and salt and sauté until the mushrooms have given up their water and have begun to deeply brown, about 12 to 15 minutes. Add garlic, ginger, and scallion whites and continue to sauté until very fragrant, about 3 to 4 minutes. If the skillet contents begin to stick, add ¼ cup of water to loosen it up.

Stir in both soy sauces, oyster sauce, and optionally liquid smoke and MSG, reduce the heat to medium-low, and allow the contents to simmer for 10 minutes. Remove from the heat.

After the rice has been soaking for an hour, uncover the Dutch oven and place over medium heat until it begins to simmer. Cover, reduce the heat to low, and allow the rice to cook until the water has been absorbed, about 5 to 6 minutes.

Uncover the pot. Pour sautéed mushrooms with sauce across the surface of the rice. Then, place tofu and chard strips around the edges of the surface. Replace the pot lid and transfer to the oven to roast for 20 minutes. Remove from the oven and let the covered pot rest for 15 minutes.

Remove the cover, garnish with scallion greens, mash it all up, and dig in! (It's okay for an eating duo to share the same pot!)

"Plov" Just Doesn't Sound Good

Uzbek carrot pilaf sounds great!

Some years back, I narrowly escaped from a burgeoning revolution in Kyrgyzstan's capital of Bishkek and hightailed it for the shores of beautiful Lake Issykkul. What a fantastic holiday. I hiked the rugged terrain surrounding the lake and found ancient glyphs, met generous local farmers, enjoyed early season cherries warm from the trees, and finally took a plunge in perhaps the coldest water in which I've ever swam. Fun fact: *Issykkul* means "hot lake." It's also the seventh deepest in the world. Creepy, black depths with great views of snowcapped mountains. Once I thawed, it was time for dinner.

This wasn't just any dinner. A buddy of mine, an Issykkul local with whom I ran from Bishkek, had a favorite eatery owned by a rather large Uzbek gentleman named Akram. He fermented his own mead. Yes, the same mead from any Arthurian legend you've ever read. It was unexpected. But not as unexpected as what I learned next. This Russian-speaking mountain of a man was also renowned for being the best vegan cook at the lake! *Plov*, Uzbekistan's national dish, is typically quite meaty, where lamb is the star. Akram's vegan answer was a shockingly rich carrot and chickpea dance that was deeply satisfying.

When he served us, he also brought over some green peas and spooned some on top with the following life lesson: *Everything is happier with peas*. We should've brought some peas back to Bishkek.

—Howie

TOTAL TIME: 1 hours, 40 minutes | **VESSEL:** 4–6 qt Dutch oven | **SERVES:** 4–6

- ¼ cup extra-virgin olive oil
- 1 onion, sliced into ¼-inch strips
- 2–3 carrots, peeled, shredded (about 1½–2 cups)
- 4 cloves garlic, minced
- 2 tsp kosher salt
- 1 tsp ground black pepper
- 1 Tbsp ground cumin
- 1 tsp ground turmeric
- 3 cups vegetable or chicken stock
- 2 (15-oz) cans chickpeas, drained and rinsed
- 1½ cups jasmine, basmati, or other long-grain white rice, uncooked

Preheat the oven to 350°F.

Add olive oil to a Dutch oven over medium heat. When the oil begins to shimmer, add onion and sauté until it has softened and begun to brown, about 8 to 10 minutes. Add carrots, garlic, salt, pepper, cumin, and turmeric, and continue to sauté for an additional 6 to 8 minutes, or until the carrots have softened but not broken. Add stock to the pot and bring to a boil. Reduce the heat to low, add chickpeas, and simmer for 30 minutes.

Distribute rice across the top of the contents of the pot and gently submerge the rice with the back of a spoon. Cover and transfer the pot to the oven for 45 minutes.

Remove the pot from the oven. Allow the plov to rest, covered, for 15 minutes. Remove the lid, stir everything together, and serve directly to bowls. Peas on top are an optional ode to Akram.

Pasta Night in One Pot?

Sign me up!

Stop me if you've already heard this tragic story of fettuccine Alfredo. Good luck with that. Despite some reports to the contrary, Alfredo is actually an Italian-born recipe for a creamy, cheesy white sauce that decadently drapes long silky noodles. Many believe that it is an Italian American invention, and it is not. The American part of the story involves the systematic destruction of a once-elegant dish first crafted by a chef of the same name. Chef Alfredo never saw the dish gain popularity among Italians, though it did arrive in the United States with Americans lucky enough to have enjoyed its brief flame in Rome.

Once Americans got ahold of the genius sauce, cream got added to make up for inaccessible and deeply flavored Italian cheeses and butter. Going commercial is what really took it down. The sauce got loaded up with floury starches to blatantly thicken it up, flying in the face of why the dish came to be in the first place. Naturally thickening Parmesan cheese and butter mixing with starchy pasta reveals the truest smooth character of Alfredo. Indeed, as I am an American cook, I also use cream because cream is delicious. Oh, also it's in one pot, which is superconvenient.

—Greg

TOTAL TIME: 45 minutes (if including bread, add 1 hour dough proof time from This Pot Lid Thing's Getting Ridiculous from page 213) | **VESSEL:** 6 qt Dutch oven | **SERVES:** 8–10

FOR THE MEATBALLS:

1 lb ground beef or turkey
1 egg
½ tsp kosher salt
½ tsp garlic powder
½ tsp onion powder
½ tsp ground black pepper
½ cup bread crumbs
¼ bunch parsley, roughly chopped
½ cup Parmesan cheese, grated or shredded

FOR THE PASTA:

½ cup butter (1 stick)
2 cups heavy cream
4 cloves garlic, minced
½ tsp ground black pepper
1 cup milk, plus more as necessary
1 lb linguine, fettuccine, or other long pasta
½ bunch parsley, roughly chopped
1 cup Parmesan cheese, grated or shredded
Roasted red pepper slices, for garnish

FOR THE BREAD (OPTIONAL):

1 recipe This Pot Lid Thing's Getting Ridiculous bread dough from page 213, uncooked

(Directions on next page)

Preheat the oven to 375°F.

To prepare the meatballs, thoroughly mix all ingredients. Form 1–1½-inch balls and place on a sheet pan. Set aside.

To prepare the pasta, add butter, cream, garlic, pepper, and 1 cup of milk to a Dutch oven over medium heat. When the butter is melted, add pasta (broken in half is easier). Bring the mixture to a boil over medium-high heat, then reduce the heat to medium-low and simmer, stirring occasionally, for 10 to 12 minutes, or until the pasta is just al dente. Stir in parsley and Parmesan. Add a bit of milk if the consistency of the sauce isn't right. Place the meatballs atop the creamy pasta. It's okay if they sink into the sauce.

If including the lid bread: Grease the underside of the Dutch oven lid with olive oil. Line the edge then the middle with seasoned dough balls. The seasoned dough balls should cover the surface of the underside of the lid. Place the upside-down lid atop the Dutch oven.

Transfer the otherwise filled pot to the oven and bake until biscuits are starting to brown, about 25 to 30 minutes. Remove the pot from the oven, carefully remove the bread-covered lid, and serve the pull-apart bread with awesome heaps of cheesy pasta and meatballs. Top with roasted red peppers for fun!

The Did You See *Big Night*? Pasta Timpano

Here we go making you flip a Dutch oven again

There are dishes that include some of your favorite things and then there are those dishes that have *all the things*. *Timpano* is one of them. But first, a bit about the title of this dish. *Timpano* flew far under the radar amid Italian cookery in the United States for decades. That is, until the eventual cult film *Big Night* came out. Long story short, two Italian brothers in early twentieth-century New York City prepare a huge meal in anticipation of singer Louis Prima visiting their little restaurant. One of these dishes is perhaps the most complex, truest celebration of Southern Italian cuisine you've ever seen.

One does not take *timpano* lightly or approach it casually on a weeknight. It has many phases and lots of techniques rolled into one long afternoon. Well ahead of this monster being fully done, you're rolling dough, making meatballs and sausage, cooking pasta, chopping madly, braising gravy, remembering to breathe, etc. You will feel like you're cooking an entire banquet, and you kind of are, but all of these favorite Italian goodies are wrapped up in one huge pastry. Once you get to that magic moment of cutting into what amounts to the best potpie ever, have a crowd around to marvel. This is your Big Night.

—Greg

TOTAL TIME: 3 hours, 45 minutes, plus prep time | **VESSEL:** 4½ qt Dutch oven | **SERVES:** 8–10

FOR THE PASTRY:

2½ ft x 2½ ft fresh pasta sheets OR
- 4 large eggs, beaten
- 3 cups flour
- 1½ Tbsp extra-virgin olive oil
- 1½ tsp kosher salt

FOR THE FILLING:

- 15 oz ricotta cheese
- 4 oz cream cheese, softened
- 10 oz mozzarella cheese, shredded, divided
- 1 cup Parmesan cheese, grated, divided
- ¼ cup chopped parsley
- 8 oz large shell pasta, cooked 7 minutes
- 28 oz Yes, Grandma, We'll Call It Gravy from page 19, or other tomato sauce, divided, plus more for serving
- 8 oz rigatoni pasta, cooked 7 minutes
- 6 oz baby spinach, sautéed
- 16 oz beef meatballs, cooked (recipe on page 19), halved
- 3 oz salami, thinly sliced
- 2 large red bell peppers, roasted, peeled, and seeded
- 5 sweet or hot Italian sausages, cooked
- 2 large onions, sliced into ¼-inch strips, caramelized
- 8 slices provolone cheese

If making pasta dough from scratch: In a stand mixer fitted with a dough hook, thoroughly combine beaten eggs, flour, olive oil, and salt. Once a tacky dough has formed, transfer from the mixer onto a flour-dusted work surface. Knead the dough,

(Directions continued on page 135)

adding flour as necessary, until a smooth, Play-Doh-like ball forms. Wrap the dough in plastic and set aside for at least 30 minutes.

In a small mixing bowl, combine ricotta, cream cheese, 4 ounces of mozzarella, ½ cup of Parmesan, and parsley. Spoon mixture into cooked pasta shells and set aside.

Spoon 1 cup of tomato gravy or sauce into a separate mixing bowl and stir in cooked rigatoni. Set aside.

Preheat the oven to 350°F.

If using scratch-made pasta dough, unwrap the dough, transfer to a flour-dusted work surface, and roll out to approximately 2 feet by 2 feet, about 1/16th of an inch thick. Grease the inside of a Dutch oven with olive oil. Lift the dough round and place atop the pot. Gently encourage the dough to settle at the bottom of the pot and flush to the insides, with plenty of overhang to seal the top.

If using store-bought fresh pasta sheets, lay them in the pot so that they cover the bottom and the sides without any gaps, with plenty of overhang to seal the top.

Begin to layer your *timpano* filling. Anything goes, but we suggest the following order: ½ of the rigatoni, spinach, meatball halves, ⅓ of the remaining sauce, mozzarella, salami, filled pasta shells, roasted peppers, ½ of the remaining sauce, sausage, caramelized onions, provolone, remaining rigatoni, remaining sauce, and Parmesan.

Use the overhanging dough to enclose the top. Place a lid on the pot and transfer to the oven and bake for 1 hour, 30 minutes.

Remove the *timpano* from the oven, remove the pot lid, and allow it to rest for at least 1 hour before unmolding, cutting into wedges, and feasting with additional sauce.

You Could Have Been Baking Your Risotto

And nobody ever told you until now

One of the top reasons that Howie and I decided to write this book is because nothing pairs better with *delicious* than *lazy*. Dutch oven cooking more often than not includes a built-in naptime. *Allow it to simmer for 45 minutes; Transfer it to the oven to braise for 2 hours; Put the chicken on low for the entire afternoon!* But, what happens when you get to a recipe that is best served by the consistent heat of a Dutch oven, but it is said to be constant work? Do you ditch it and put on a stew? No, you find a way around the work!

Risotto, they say, needs to be coddled, stirred consistently and lovingly, introducing liquids slowly over time to gingerly extract precious starches from each grain of delicate rice, yielding a smooth, creamy mouthfeel reminiscent of silk. No. It doesn't. Those same starches are going to come off the rice and remain in the same bath, yielding something damned close to stirring for 40 minutes. Sure, you give it a good thorough mix at the penultimate stage, but c'mon, what would you sacrifice for a nap? Nobody will be the wiser.

—Greg

TOTAL TIME: 1 hour, 15 minutes | **VESSEL:** 3–5 qt Dutch oven | **SERVES:** 6–8

- 4 Tbsp extra-virgin olive oil, divided
- 4 oz sun-dried tomatoes, thinly sliced
- 4 oz roasted red peppers, sliced into ¼-inch strips
- 2 cloves garlic, minced
- 1 cup dry white wine
- 6 cups chicken or vegetable stock, divided
- 2 cups arborio, carnaroli, or other short-grain rice
- 1 cup Parmesan cheese, grated, plus more for garnish
- 1 tsp kosher salt
- ½ tsp ground black pepper
- 1 cup canned peas, drained, or frozen peas, thawed

Preheat the oven to 350°F.

Heat 2 tablespoons of olive oil in a Dutch oven over medium heat. When the oil begins to shimmer, add sun-dried tomatoes, peppers, and garlic and sauté for 4 minutes. Add wine, increase the heat to medium-high, bring to a simmer, and allow the wine to reduce by half, about 4 to 6 minutes. Add 5 cups of stock and bring to a simmer. Stir in rice, place the lid on the pot, and transfer to the oven for 50 minutes.

Remove the pot from the oven, remove the lid, and stir in Parmesan, salt, pepper, peas, one remaining cup of stock, and 2 remaining tablespoons of olive oil. Replace the lid and allow the risotto to rest for 10 minutes before re-stirring and serving loving heapfuls. Garnish with additional Parmesan as desired.

Thanksgiving in a Pot

All of the holiday hits in every forkful

Yeah, I can be a real stickler for food terminology, just open nearly any recipe introduction in this book! But when it comes to Thanksgiving "stuffing," the word gives me all the right feels even though it's no longer popular to *stuff* it in a bird. I will always use quotes, however. And don't get me started on using the word "dressing" to describe the dish. There is so much wrong with it, I just have to stop right here, in mid-sente. . .

Anyhow, I'm also the guy at the Thanksgiving table—like many of you, I'm sure—who will opt for a mountain of "stuffing," eschewing every other dish on the board. Sure, I'll take a token scoop of mashed potatoes, and a green bean or two, maybe a shred of turkey? But "stuffing" is just so perfect in every way that I often hesitate to otherwise devote plate real estate. I realize that this may seem boring to some, perhaps one-note on a day that's supposed to be about gorging on 15 casseroles within exactly 12 minutes before racing for the last couch cushion. What if I told you that you can have it all and still remain your "stuffing"-obsessed self?

(By the way, I got the last couch cushion.)

—Howie

TOTAL TIME: 2 hours, 30 minutes | **VESSEL:** 4½–6 qt Dutch oven | **SERVES:** 10–12

- 1½ lb loaf crusty bread, cut into 1-inch cubes
- 1 Tbsp butter
- 3 Tbsp extra-virgin olive oil, divided
- 1 lb cured turkey andouille or other cured sausage, diced
- 1 large onion, diced
- 6 ribs celery, diced
- 1 sweet potato, diced
- 1 lb ground turkey
- 2 tsp salt, divided
- 1 tsp ground black pepper
- 1 tsp garlic powder
- 1 Tbsp dried oregano
- 1 cup parsley, roughly chopped, divided
- ¾ cup dried cranberries
- 4 cups turkey or chicken stock

Preheat the oven to 350°F.

Place bread cubes on a sheet pan and transfer to the oven. Toast the bread for 10 minutes or until dried out but not browned. Remove the bread from the oven and set aside.

In a skillet, melt butter with 2 tablespoons of olive oil. Over medium heat, sauté the sausage until browned, about 2 to 3 minutes. Using a slotted spoon, remove the sausage to a paper towel–lined plate. Add 1 tablespoon of olive oil, onion, celery, and sweet potato to the pot and sauté until the onion is translucent, about 6 to 8 minutes. Add ground turkey, 1 teaspoon of salt, and remaining seasonings and continue to sauté until the turkey is no longer pink, about 2 to 3 minutes. Transfer the contents to a large mixing bowl and wipe out the Dutch oven. To the mixing bowl, add half of the

(Directions continued on next page)

parsley, cranberries, browned sausage, and 1 remaining teaspoon of salt, and evenly fold in reserved bread cubes.

Using a paper towel or pastry brush, coat the bottom and sides of the Dutch oven with the remaining 1 tablespoon of olive oil. Scrape the bread mixture into the pot and make sure it is evenly distributed across the surface, no bread hills.

Slowly pour the stock evenly over the mixture in the pot, being sure that some of the liquid reaches most, if not all, of the bread. Use a clean hand, the back of a wooden spoon, or spatula to gently compress the whole mixture to ensure that the liquid is evenly distributed.

Allow it to sit on the counter for an hour, undisturbed.

Transfer the pot to the oven. Roast for 50 to 60 minutes, or until the top is beginning to brown and get crusty. If the top begins to brown sooner, place the lid on the pot.

Remove the pot from the oven and allow it to rest for 5 to 10 minutes before serving, garnished with remaining parsley.

"Scalloped" Potatoes Bother Us

Do they bother you, too?

I've always enjoyed *gratin Dauphinois* as both a delectable potato dish as well as the only French term I pronounce perfectly. Listen closely, *daw-feen-wah*. Beautiful. If you're not familiar, gratin Dauphinois is essentially the grandmother of old-school American scalloped potatoes, minus the America-defining cheese layers. But, can we talk about scallops for a moment? Yes, that's right, scallops, the *seafood*. How does a potato dish earn the name of a mollusk? Did the dish once contain this delicious shellfish? Did the shape of the cut spud give its name to this round white sea creature? Confusingly none of the above.

There are a few theories in the world, but the two most popular are, 1) the dish is named using the French "escalope," which is usually allocated for thin slices of meat; and 2) the dish was first cooked in a scallop shell. Where do I begin? You want me to believe that the French would ever demean a word for sliced meat to be assigned to a vegetable dish? You alternatively want me to believe that a scallop shell has ever been large enough to accommodate enough potato slices to feed even one hungry mouth? Folks, I don't have an answer for this. Rename this dish and let us know what you come up with. Thanks.

—Greg

TOTAL TIME: 2 hours | **VESSEL:** 3+ qt Dutch oven | **SERVES:** 6–8

- 3 cups half-and-half or cream
- 3 large eggs
- 2 tsp salt
- 1 tsp ground black pepper
- 1 tsp garlic powder
- 1 tsp onion powder
- 1 tsp ancho or other chile powder
- 1 Tbsp dried oregano
- 3 Tbsp extra-virgin olive oil, divided
- 1½ lb russet potatoes, peeled, sliced ⅛-inch thick (a mandoline helps)
- 1½ lb sweet potatoes, peeled, sliced ⅛-inch thick
- 3 cups sharp cheese

Preheat the oven to 375°F.

In a large mixing bowl, whisk together half-and-half or cream, eggs, salt, pepper, garlic powder, onion powder, chile powder, and oregano. Using a pastry brush or paper towel, coat the bottom and sides of a Dutch oven with 1 tablespoon of olive oil.

As you slice the potatoes, place them in the egg/cream mixture to keep them from discoloring. In the pot, form a layer using ⅓ of the russet and sweet potato slices, overlapping them like shingles. Sprinkle 1 cup of cheese over the potatoes. Repeat with another layer of ⅓ of the potato slices, then 1 cup of cheese. Place one last layer of the remaining sweet and russet potato slices, but hold off on the cheese.

Slowly pour the cream mixture over the potatoes, giving it some time to fall to the bottom of the baking dish and surround its contents. Sprinkle the remaining cheese across the top.

(Directions continued on next page)

Place a lid on the Dutch oven, transfer to the oven, and bake for 1 hour, 15 minutes. Remove the pot from the oven, remove the lid, and return to the oven for an additional 20 to 25 minutes or until the top cheese begins to brown.

Remove the "scalloped" potatoes from the oven and allow it to cool for 10 to 15 minutes before slicing and serving warm.

Arroz con Pollo

A truly globalized chicken and rice

If you do an internet search for chicken and rice, chances are the first several entries will present recipes and/or history of arroz con pollo, Spanish for chicken and rice. This is pretty weird, considering the chicken and the rice both came from decidedly non-Spanish-speaking lands. Chicken was first domesticated in India and rice was first cultivated in China. Funny story, both of these places have their own version of chicken and rice that fail to show up in the first (several?) hundred search results: Chicken biryani from Northern India and Hainan chicken and rice from Southern China. Both outstanding and worthy of popping up on your favorite browser!

Howie and I have traveled the globe in search of the best, the brightest, and the most accessible chicken and rice recipes. We must admit, versions from Central and South America and those from the Mediterranean—often titled arroz con pollo—are really very good. Perhaps even better than our Asian favorites. *Say it isn't so!* So, to meet everyone in the middle, we accept the Spanish title, but we've also distilled the dish to maintain an undeniable melting-pot vibe.

—Greg

TOTAL TIME: 1½ hours | Equipment: 6 qt Dutch oven | **SERVES:** 4–6

- 1 whole chicken, cut into 8 pieces
- 3 tsp salt, divided
- ½ tsp ground black pepper
- 4 tsp vegetable oil, divided
- 2 cups long-grain white rice, uncooked
- 2 onions, chopped
- 2 red bell peppers, chopped
- 1 green bell pepper, chopped
- 4 cloves garlic, chopped
- 2 Tbsp tomato paste
- 2 tsp paprika
- 2 tsp chile powder
- ½ tsp turmeric
- 3 cups chicken stock or broth
- 10 green olives
- 1 cup frozen peas
- ½ cup cilantro, roughly chopped

Preheat oven to 375°F. Rub the chicken with 1 teaspoon of salt and ½ teaspoon of pepper. Heat 2 teaspoons oil in a Dutch oven over medium-high heat until the oil shimmers, about 1 minute. Place the chicken in the oven, skin-side down, and let it fry for 3 to 4 minutes, until golden brown.

Turn the chicken, and continue to brown all sides, about 6 to 8 minutes total. Remove the chicken from the skillet. Add rice into the skillet, tossing it and coating it with the rendered fat from the chicken. Stir for about 3 minutes until aromatic and very lightly brown. Remove the rice from the skillet.

Add 2 teaspoons oil and heat over medium heat until shimmering. Add onions, and sauté for 6 to 8 minutes until translucent. Add the pepper, garlic, and the remaining 2 teaspoons salt. Gently sauté for 4 to 6 minutes. Add tomato paste, paprika, chile powder, and turmeric, and stir to coat the vegetables. Sauté another minute, until aromatic.

(Directions continued on page 145)

Add the rice back into the skillet, stirring until coated. Immediately pour in the chicken stock or broth and scrape the bottom of the pot with a spoon to release all the browned bits. Bring to a light simmer and nestle the chicken into the top of the rice. Cover and place in the oven for 20 minutes.

Remove the skillet from the oven and add the olives and peas. Place the cover back on and return to the oven for an additional 20 minutes.

Top with cilantro and serve.

Ziti the Way Nature Intended

With ricotta, too many peppers, and a ton of mozz

When I was a kid, baked ziti always seemed like something you made with leftovers. We'd come back home from a Sunday at my grandparents' with a leftover pound of rigatoni, too many meatballs and sausages to count, and what had to be a quart of gravy. Monday night meant breaking up the meaty components, shredding some mozzarella, and mixing it all with a container of ricotta, the overage of pasta, and all that lovely gravy. Chewy top, crispy edges, creamy interior with perfectly coordinated hunks of meat.

As an adult with a wife who appreciates a great gravy and kids who go to town on pasta night, hardly anything is left for baked ziti the next day. So, now it tends to be a freshly made dish, axing the meat—as long as my doctor is reading this—and adding punchy roasted red peppers. Of course, there is the allure of a leftover noodle that soaked up every bit of sauce overnight. Tell you what—cook it tonight and eat it tomorrow. Bang.

—Howie

TOTAL TIME: 1 hour | **VESSEL:** 4½–6 qt Dutch oven | **SERVES:** 8–10

- 4 qt water
- 1 lb rigatoni or penne pasta
- 2 Tbsp, plus 1 tsp kosher salt, divided
- 20 oz Yes, Grandma, We'll Call It Gravy from page 19, or other tomato sauce, cooled
- 2 cups ricotta cheese
- 10 oz roasted red peppers, sliced into ¼-inch strips
- 1 cup Parmesan cheese, shredded or grated
- 1 lb mozzarella, shredded
- 2 Tbsp extra-virgin olive oil

Preheat oven to 400°F.

In a large pot, bring water to a rolling boil over high heat. Add pasta and 2 tablespoons of salt. Cook for 10 minutes, stirring occasionally to ensure the pasta does not stick to the pot. Drain the pasta and in a colander over the sink, rinse with cold water to stop the cooking, and set aside.

In a large mixing bowl, thoroughly combine cooked pasta with tomato gravy or sauce, ricotta, peppers, Parmesan, ¾ of the mozzarella, and 1 remaining teaspoon of salt.

Using a paper towel or pastry brush, coat the bottom and sides of a Dutch oven with the olive oil. Scrape the pasta mixture from the mixing bowl into the pot, and top with the remaining ¼ of mozzarella. Transfer to the oven and bake uncovered for 35 to 40 minutes, or until the cheese on top is golden brown. Allow the ziti to rest for 10 minutes before serving hot. Or, leave it to cool, cover, and pop it in the fridge and rewarm the next day. Intentional leftovers.

Chilla-Killas!

A really fun way to title a tortilla casserole!

When most folks consider tortillas and their typical applications, the list is pretty short: tacos, burritos, enchiladas, quesadillas, and of course, chips and dip. But there are entire schools of tortilla-based cooking that go well beyond. Tortilla as a soup thickener is genius. Tortilla as a dredge for frying is stupendous. Tortillas as a base for pizza-like Tlayuda! Here, take my money! Amid all of these great alternatives for the humble tortilla, there is one clear winner for me and that is slightly stewing crispy tortillas in a savory sauce!

Chilaquiles is a warming and unique Mexican concoction of crispy tortillas bathing in a tomato pepper sauce, all blanketed by melty cheese and eggs that roast on the top. This may well be the breakfast of champions. Bonus points for the texture of the tortilla chips alone—otherworldly. But, as a complete package, it does the job of providing vitamins, carbohydrates, calcium, and protein. I'm not going to claim chilaquiles are a health food. I'm just suggesting that health food can learn a thing or two from chilaquiles.

—Greg

TOTAL TIME: 35 minutes | **VESSEL:** 3+ qt Dutch oven | **SERVES:** 4–6

- 1 (28-oz) can tomatoes
- 2 red bell peppers, roasted, peeled, seeded
- ½ red onion
- 5 cloves garlic
- 1 tsp ground black pepper
- 1 tsp ground cumin
- 3 tsp kosher salt, divided
- 1 cup water
- 10 oz Monterey jack cheese, shredded
- 8 oz thick tortilla chips
- 6–8 eggs
- 1 large avocado, diced
- Cilantro leaves for garnish

In blender, puree tomatoes, peppers, onion, garlic, black pepper, cumin, and 2 teaspoons of salt. Pour puree and water into a Dutch oven over medium-high heat. Bring the mixture to a boil. Reduce the heat to low and simmer for 20 minutes.

Preheat the oven to broil.

Stir in half of the cheese until almost blended in, about 4 to 6 minutes. Turn off the heat and stir in tortilla chips. It's fine if some of them break up. Place individually cracked eggs atop the submerged tortilla chips, sprinkle with remaining salt, and transfer the pot to the oven. Broil until the egg whites have cooked and the yolk is still runny, about 3 to 4 minutes.

Garnish with diced avocado and cilantro and serve immediately. Black beans are a traditional accompaniment to chilaquiles.

Pan con Tomate

Life-changing simplicity

Apart from quick trips to Italy, England, and Switzerland, I had never before thought about living in Europe. I'm the guy who travels to China whenever I have the time and money. So, when my wife came home from work one day and asked if we'd ever consider moving to Barcelona, of course I said, "Sounds great!" What else was I going to say? Honestly, I had no idea of what to expect, especially from a food perspective. I had only internet listicles of the "Top Ten Dishes You Must Eat in Spain." They were always the same ten things, so I wasn't particularly intrigued by Spanish cuisine. Then, I unpacked my bags in what is now my new #2 food country.

As it turns out, those "Top Ten Dishes" hardly scratched the surface. It left me wondering why creamy rice, melon soup, and tuna tartare never make the list, but paella, gazpacho, and garlic shrimp have been there forever. All this being said, one item on the Top Ten list—that doesn't sound like much—changed my life entirely: *Pan con tomate*, or tomato bread. Believe it or not, there is great debate over the right bread, the proper level of tomato ripeness, and the order in which the olive oil, grated tomato, and salt hit the toast. Every place has a signature style, and there is indeed great diversity of experience in eating it. I know it sounds boring. It appears to be boring. It feels like it's going to be boring. Friends. It's not boring.

For you, and to add to its inherent diversity, I brought it back to the States and casseroled it.

—Howie

TOTAL TIME: 1 hour | **VESSEL:** 4½ qt Dutch oven | **SERVES:** 6–8

1 lb crusty bread, diced
1¼–1½ lb tomatoes, halved, grated, skins discarded
2 tsp kosher salt
2 eggs
10 Tbsp extra-virgin olive oil, divided

Preheat the oven to 375°F.

Place diced bread on a sheet pan and toast in the oven until lightly toasted, about 8 to 10 minutes. While the bread toasts, in a large mixing bowl, whisk together grated tomatoes, salt, eggs, and 4 tablespoons of olive oil. When the bread is toasted, remove it from the oven and fold it into the tomato mixture.

Grease a Dutch oven using 2 tablespoons of olive oil. Evenly pour tomato-bread mixture into the pot. Using the back of a spoon or a clean hand, press the mixture flat. Drizzle the top with the remaining 4 tablespoons of olive oil. Transfer the pot to the oven and bake until the top is just beginning to get brown and crusty, about 40 to 50 minutes.

Remove the casserole from the oven and enjoy it as a side while piping hot.

Arroz Verde

Do they celebrate St. Patty's Day in Mexico?

Cilantro is a great little leaf. Vegetal, crisp, and clean, even a little bit sprinkled over eggs or in a salad can completely transform and transcend. Unless you are unlucky enough to have the gene variant that makes it taste like someone dropped a small bowl of dish soap into your ceviche.

If you hate cilantro, just skip this dish. More for the rest of us!

—Greg

TOTAL TIME: 30 min | **VESSEL:** 3 qt Dutch oven | **SERVES:** 6–8 as a side dish

1 (7-oz) can fire-roasted green peppers
½ white onion, chopped
2 cloves garlic, chopped or pressed
2 tsp salt
½ tsp cumin
1 cup cilantro, chopped
2 tsp oil
2 cups long-grain white rice
3 cups water
Juice of 1 lime

Place the green peppers, onion, garlic, salt, cumin, and half of the cilantro in a blender, and puree for about 1 minute, or until completely smooth

Heat oil in a Dutch oven over medium-high heat. When the oil begins to shimmer, add the rice, and stir well to coat. Cook the rice for 3 to 5 minutes, stirring occasionally. When some of the grains are a deeper white and a few are starting to brown, pour in the water and pureed pepper mixture. Stir to combine well.

Bring the mixture to a boil, and then turn the heat to a low simmer. Cover and cook for 20 minutes, until the rice is completely cooked through. Turn off the heat and pour in the lime juice. Cover and allow to rest for another 5 minutes.

Pour the rice into a bowl and mix with the remaining ½ cup of cilantro. Add a bit more salt and/or lime to taste. Goes well with any spicy dish.

What Happens When a Pizzaiolo Goes Nuts?

Mangled meat-lovers' pizza

Howie wrote the introduction below and recipe for a previous book and I updated the recipe to be much, much better. The intro was solid and didn't need anything. It's perfect. Still, you should buy our previous books so you can check to see if I am right about the recipe. I'll wait here and think about how to improve this recipe yet again in future books. It's fine, I have plenty of time. Trust me, go on.

—Greg

"The one problem with pizza is that it's just too neat, too put together. No one and no food is that organized. Pizza should reflect life and embody a reality that we're all dealing with. Troubles at work? Bills to pay? Dog jumping on the guests? Glasses prescription getting worse? Hair thinning quickly? *My aching back!?* But, I digress. This is, finally, a (de)construction of pizza that will make you feel like your life is relatively tidy."

—Howie

TOTAL TIME: 2 hours, 15 minutes | **VESSEL:** 4–5 qt Dutch oven | **SERVES:** 6–8

- 1 lb crusty bread, cubed
- 1 tsp kosher salt
- ½ tsp ground black pepper
- 1 Tbsp dried oregano
- 2 tsp onion powder
- 2 tsp garlic powder
- 1 cup Parmesan cheese, grated or shredded, divided
- 6 oz Italian sausage, casing removed, cooked
- 8 oz meatballs, sliced
- 6 oz pepperoni, diced
- 1 lb fresh mozzarella, diced
- 5 eggs
- 1 cup milk
- 2 cups Yes, Grandma, We'll Call It Gravy (page 19), or other tomato sauce
- 2 Tbsp extra-virgin olive oil, divided

Preheat the oven to 375°F.

Place the bread cubes on a sheet pan and toast in the oven for 10 minutes.

In a large mixing bowl, toss the bread cubes with salt, pepper, oregano, onion powder, garlic powder, and ½ cup Parmesan. Stir in the meats.

Evenly pour ½ of the bread mixture into a Dutch oven. Top with ½ of the mozzarella. Then, pour the remaining bread mixture atop the cheese. Be sure you have one even layer with a flat top (no bread hills).

In a separate mixing bowl, whisk together eggs, milk, and gravy or sauce. Slowly pour the egg mixture evenly over the bread mixture, being sure that some of the liquid reaches most, if not all, of the bread. Use the back of a wooden spoon, a clean hand, or spatula to compress the whole mixture to ensure that the liquid is evenly distributed. Distribute the remaining mozzarella and Parmesan across the top.

Place a lid on the pot and allow it to sit for an hour before baking. Transfer the pot to the oven and bake for 30 minutes. Carefully remove the lid and continue to bake for another 25 to 30 minutes, or until the top is beginning to brown and get crusty.

Remove the mangled pizza from the oven and allow it to cool for 10 minutes before scooping hot maddening joy.

A Jambalaya Walks into a Spanish Bar

A rice casserole for the Iberian-Cajun inside all of us

I love jambalaya and versions of the Cajun and Creole classic has appeared in our other books. There is so much possibility with the format that it has made sense to me over the years to try to take another step forward without losing the spirit of the dish. I discovered a way to change the game through which the rice retains its own identity, the vegetables sing, and creatures from land and sea cook perfectly. Perhaps strangely, the answer to my reinvention of jambalaya hails from Spain.

In Spanish cuisine, if a dish involves rice, rice is the undeniable star of the show. If it's paella, the rice layer is thin, the bottom crispy, the middle creamy, and the top toasty with meaty footnotes. If it's *arroz meloso*, the rice and liquid meld to a silky texture that would make any risotto jealous. If it's *arroz caldoso*, the rice, now delicate, swims in a decadent pool of flavor. So, as I'm thinking of ways to innovate atop jambalaya, my first priority was to have whole bites of rice with hints of meaty flavor seeped in. Second priority was to present whole bites of meat and seafood. The third priority was to allow for a spoonful of mixed rice-y rice *and* meaty goodness.

It worked. This layered version of jambalaya hits all the traditional notes and yet finishes in a very Spanish way. The individual parts survive, where typical jambalaya loses them all to a nebulous mush.

—Howie

TOTAL TIME: 2 hours | **VESSEL:** 4½ qt Dutch oven | **SERVES:** 8–10

- 2 cups jasmine or other long-grain rice, uncooked
- 2 cups All the Bones Broth from page 93, or chicken stock
- 1 lb seafood of choice: peeled shrimp, calamari rings, bay scallops, etc.
- 2 tsp kosher salt, divided
- 3 tsp ground cumin, divided
- 3 tsp smoked paprika, divided
- ¼ cup extra-virgin olive oil
- 1 lb Spanish chorizo or other smoked sausage, sliced into ¼-inch rounds
- 2 onions, thinly sliced
- ½ bunch celery, diced
- 1 Tbsp dried oregano
- 8 cloves garlic, roughly chopped
- 1 large red bell pepper, roasted, peeled, seeded, sliced into ¼-inch strips
- 3 Tbsp tomato paste
- ⅔ cup water
- 4 scallions, thinly sliced

In a mixing bowl, rinse the rice until the water runs nearly clear, about 3 to 4 times. Place drained rice and 2 cups of broth or stock in a Dutch oven, off the heat. Cover and set aside for 1 hour.

Preheat the oven to 350°F.

(Directions continued on next page)

In a mixing bowl, combine seafood with ½ teaspoon salt, 1 teaspoon cumin, and 1 teaspoon paprika. Set aside.

Add oil to a separate skillet over medium-high heat. Add sausage and sauté until browned, 3 to 4 minutes. Using a slotted spoon, remove sausage from the pan and set aside. Reduce the heat to medium-low and add onions and celery. Sauté until the onions are very soft and dark tan in color, about 30 to 40 minutes.

Add the remaining 2 teaspoons each of cumin and paprika as well as the remaining 1½ teaspoons salt and stir to combine. Add oregano, garlic, roasted pepper, and tomato paste and continue to sauté until fragrant, about 3 to 4 minutes. Turn off the heat and stir in water and browned sausage.

After the rice has been soaking for an hour, uncover the Dutch oven and place over medium-high heat until it begins to simmer. Cover, reduce the heat to low, and allow the rice to cook until the water has been absorbed, about 6 to 8 minutes.

Uncover the pot. Pour onion-sausage mixture from the skillet across the surface of the rice. Then, top with seasoned seafood. Replace the pot lid and transfer to the oven to roast for 25 minutes. Remove from the oven and let the covered pot rest for 20 minutes.

Remove the cover, garnish with scallion greens, stir it all up, and eat!

Seriously Tall Eggplant Parm

A ridiculously proportioned take on the classic

By now you may have guessed that I judge a diner by its corned beef hash, a Spanish bar by its tuna tartare, a Chinese place by its steamed buns, and a brasserie by its cassoulet. If these items are great, the rest of their menus are probably solid. It's also probably not a huge leap to suppose I judge an Italian American joint by its eggplant Parmesan. If the chef does this well, their pasta dishes are likely divine, their fish sublime, and their meatballs delicious. I'm probably being overly general about what makes a restaurant great, but hey, we all have our thing.

There is some logic to my shallow method of assessment. I pick a dish that can be finessed and choices are made that either make or kill a recipe for me. If certain choices are made the way I would make them in the kitchen, then the place is probably sharing my wavelengths and I will enjoy their cooking.

Specific to eggplant parm, I was raised to believe that A) the fruit—yes, fruit—is peeled, sliced into rounds, then dredged in flour, egg, then fine bread crumbs and shallow fried; B) Sunday gravy is the foundation of all eggplant parm goodness; and C) more cheese is better cheese. When presented with the Dutch oven as a vessel to make eggplant history, I added D) a monster version was coming soon.

—Howie

TOTAL TIME: 1 hour, 30 minutes | **VESSEL:** 3–4½ qt Dutch oven | **SERVES:** 6–8

- 1½ cup flour
- 3 eggs, lightly beaten
- 2 Tbsp water
- 2½ cups bread crumbs
- 3 tsp kosher salt, divided
- 2 large Italian eggplants, peeled, and cut into ¼-inch rounds
- 2–3 cups canola or vegetable oil
- 20 oz Yes, Grandma, We'll Call It Gravy from page 19, or other tomato sauce, cooled
- 3 Tbsp extra-virgin olive oil
- 1 tsp black pepper
- 2 tsp dried oregano
- 2 lb mozzarella cheese, shredded
- 1 cup Parmesan cheese, shredded or grated

Preheat the oven to 375°F. Using three shallow bowls, set up a dredging station. In the first bowl, place the flour. In the second bowl, whisk together the eggs and water. In the third bowl, mix the bread crumbs with 2 tsp of salt. Place a clean plate at the end of the dredging station. Dip one eggplant round into the all-purpose flour, and shake off excess. Then, dip the eggplant into the egg mixture, let excess drip away. Then, dip it into the bread crumbs to coat and place on the plate. Repeat with the remainder of the eggplant and set the plate aside.

Pour enough canola or vegetable oil in a skillet to about ¾-inch in depth. Heat the oil to 360°F over medium heat. If you do not have a thermometer, one handy trick is to use a wooden chopstick, like the kind you get with Chinese takeout. As the oil heats, touch the tip of the chopstick to the bottom of the skillet at

(Directions continued on page 161)

an angle. Once you see bubbles forming around the entirety of the submerged chopstick, the oil is ready.

Prepare a wire rack over a baking sheet and place next to the skillet. Carefully place a few coated eggplant rounds into the hot oil at a time, being sure not to overcrowd the skillet. Flip each round when the bottom has been fried to golden brown, about 1½ to 2 minutes. After another 1½ to 2 minutes, the eggplant rounds are done and can be removed to the wire rack. Pour the oil into a steel bowl and set aside to cool before discarding.

Coat the bottom of a Dutch oven with ½ cup of the tomato sauce. Form one layer of slightly overlapping fried eggplant rounds on top of the tomato sauce. Spoon tomato sauce on top of the layer, then top them with mozzarella, using about 1/5 of the shreds and then a sprinkling of Parmesan. Continue to build layers of eggplant, sauce, mozzarella, and Parmesan until you have none left. Use good judgment to end up with none of each.

Roast in the oven for 45 to 60 minutes, or until the top is bubbly and dark brown in spots. Serve deep, deep slices with non-deep-fried sides and a pasta, or on sandwiches.

Grown-Up Mac and Cheese

The name speaks for itself

I guess this is pretty typical, but my kids adore mac and cheese. They graduated from the boxed version pretty early on. As a professional cook, that pleased me. The boys actually end up being some of the best consultants on some fairly complex recipes. As they've grown, naturally, their palates have gotten better. This opened up the floodgates for spice combinations and cheeses that would have made the average 4-year-old cower. This recipe simply tastes grown up. The addition of provolone and Parmesan are game changers on their own. Imagine what happens when Asiago comes to the party.

By the way, salmon sashimi and hot sauce are pretty intense for an 11-year-old and a 9-year-old, right? Don't worry, my kids are also normal and have their least favorite things. But, given what I do for a living, it drives me up the wall that mashed potatoes and English muffins are among the hated foods in my household. *How does anybody hate mashed potatoes and English muffins? How does that happen!?*

—Howie

TOTAL TIME: 1 hour, 10 minutes | **VESSEL:** 3–4 qt Dutch oven | **SERVES:** 6–8

- 3 quarts water
- 1 lb dry macaroni
- 3 Tbsp, plus 1 tsp kosher salt
- 2 eggs
- 1 cup heavy cream
- 1 cup milk
- 1 cup sour cream
- ½ cup cream cheese, softened
- 1 tsp sweet or hot paprika
- 1 tsp ground black pepper
- ½ tsp garlic powder
- ½ tsp onion powder
- 1 tsp red chile flakes (optional)
- 1 Tbsp dried oregano
- 4 cups (about 12 oz) Asiago, cheddar, provolone, Parmesan, or other mixed cheeses, shredded, divided
- 2 Tbsp extra-virgin olive oil, divided
- ⅓ cup bread crumbs

Preheat the oven to 375°F. In a large pasta pot, bring water to a rolling boil over high heat. Add pasta and 3 tablespoons of salt. Cook for 10 minutes, stirring occasionally to ensure the pasta does not stick to the pot. Drain the pasta in a colander, and rinse with cold water to stop it from cooking further. Be sure the pasta is drained completely.

While the pasta cooks, in a large mixing bowl, whisk together eggs, cream, milk, sour cream, cream cheese, the spices, and the remaining 1 teaspoon of salt. Add in the drained pasta and 3 cups of the shredded cheese and mix thoroughly.

Coat the bottom and sides of a Dutch oven with 1 tablespoon of olive oil. Pour the pasta mixture into the pot. In a small mixing bowl, mix the remaining cup of cheese with bread crumbs and one remaining tablespoon of olive oil. Top the macaroni mixture with the bread crumb/cheese mixture. Place the uncovered pot into the oven and bake for 40 to 50 minutes. The cheese on top should be bubbly and starting to brown.

Try to include some of the chewy top with each spooned serving.

Springing a Leek

Soufflés are springy

My mom says that my dad was the only human ever to gain weight during chemo. My sister and I proudly take the blame. As does this, his favorite dish.

His course of treatment required him to sit in a hospital isolation room for a month, as his immune system was systematically destroyed and rebuilt. It was pretty miserable. So, we decided to make it a bit less miserable by bringing him lunch every day. And we ate every meal as if it were our last. Pastramis, burgers, *and* chili dogs. You want fries *and* onion rings with that? Yes, please.

But, his favorite dish? The one that he could devour in the depths of his treatment when he became too weary to lift a cheesesteak to his lips? With no energy or appetite? My sister Alicia's leek soufflé. This dish transcends.

I don't know if this story makes the dish sound delicious. I mean, you don't often see cancer used to whet your appetite. But it's an amazing dish. Trust me. Trust my sister. Trust my dad.

—Greg

TOTAL TIME: 30 minutes | **VESSEL:** 4½+ qt Dutch oven | **SERVES:** 4–6

- 8 Tbsp butter (1 stick), divided
- 2 large leeks, (whites and light green only), halved lengthwise, washed, sliced into ¼-inch strips
- 1 tsp salt
- ½ tsp pepper
- ½ tsp ground nutmeg
- 10 eggs
- 2 cups heavy cream
- 2 cups sharp cheddar cheese, shredded

Preheat the oven to 350°F.

In a Dutch oven over medium heat, melt all but ½ tablespoon of the butter. When the butter is melted, and just beginning to bubble, turn the heat down to low and add the leeks. Allow the leeks to cook for 15 minutes, stirring occasionally. When the leeks are soft, turn off the heat and add the salt, pepper, and nutmeg. Stir to combine, and reserve in a bowl.

In a separate bowl, beat the eggs with the cream until combined and a bit frothy. Add the cheese and the leek mixture into the bowl and stir to combine. Take the reserved ½ tablespoon of butter and grease the sides of the Dutch oven. Pour the leek and cheese mixture into the Dutch oven, and place in the oven, uncovered, for 45 minutes, or until the egg in the center is fully cooked.

Remove from the oven and serve warm. This dish is also delicious reheated the next day.

Penne for Your Thoughts

Artichokes, capers, and mozzarella to soothe the mind

If I were to tell you of Ciro "The Artichoke King" Terranova, you'd probably imagine that I was referring to the man who brought artichokes to California. Or maybe the guy who figured out how to process and bottle an artichoke heart. But, no such luck. Ciro Terranova was a New York mobster with one of the oddest stories you'll ever run into.

It turns out that he made his name and his money by cornering the New York market on California Artichokes. He forced growers to sell to him at his named price, under threat of violence. And he did the same with sellers in New York—from grocery stores to corner pushcarts, every choke in the five boroughs was under the control of "The Artichoke King." It got so bad that, for a time in 1935, Mayor La Guardia outlawed the artichoke!

Well, let's celebrate the triumph of open competition and the downfall of vegetable rackets with this fantastic weeknight one-pot crowd pleaser. *Grazie!*

—Greg

TOTAL TIME: 1 hour | **VESSEL:** 3 qt Dutch oven | **SERVES:** 3–4

- 1 pound penne
- 1 Tbsp olive oil
- 1 pound boneless, skinless chicken breast, sliced into ¼-inch strips
- ½ tsp salt
- 4 cloves garlic, minced
- 14 oz. bottle of artichoke hearts, drained
- 3 Tbsp capers
- ½ pound mozzarella, shredded

Preheat the oven to 350°F.

In a large pot of salted water, boil the penne until just underdone, about 3 minutes less time than the box recommends.

While the penne is boiling, heat olive oil in a Dutch oven over medium-high heat. When the oil begins to shimmer, add the chicken and salt, and sauté for 6 to 8 minutes, until the chicken is fully white. Add the garlic and continue to sauté for about 1 minute, or until fragrant. Turn off the heat, and add the artichokes and capers.

When the pasta is ready, drain and add it to the pot. Add the shredded cheese, and toss everything until it is all mixed up. Place in the oven, uncovered, for 40 minutes.

Beef Stroganoff

It's what's for breakfast

Russia was not top of mind when I'd think of where to go for my next vacation. So, when I had a work opportunity to teach a course, my wife decided to hop on board and we'd add a week and take a look around. Having grown up in the 70s and 80s, to stand in Red Square would be so weird (it was). Seeing as how we travel for food, Russia provided a particular challenge, and we were ready to dig deep and find the culinary gems. Funny thing about Russia, if breakfast eateries do exist, they are hidden. That is, except if we wanted to cave and eat an egg McMuffin (we didn't). So, we walked, and walked, and walked, got hungry, then we got *hangry*. It was suddenly 10:00 a.m. and we were withered versions of our former selves.

Just before Saint Petersburg had the chance to break us, a bar and grill appeared out of nowhere. And it was *OPEN*. Correction: The place was empty and I don't think it was actually open for business though the door was open as we entered. It may have been our desperate, disheveled look, but a kindly server who obviously just turned up to prep for the real opening hours at noon offered to see what was in the kitchen already prepared. We gladly accepted, and frankly the mystery of what would come out of the kitchen added requisite intrigue to our Russian adventure. You already know where this is going. Beef Stroganoff never tasted better than it did that day, my friends. Admittedly, however, the version below tries hard.

—Howie

TOTAL TIME: 1 hour, 40 minutes | **VESSEL:** 3+ qt Dutch oven | **SERVES:** 6–8

- 5 Tbsp butter, divided
- 1–1½ lb beef chuck roast, cut into ½-inch strips
- 2 tsp kosher salt, divided
- 1 large onion, diced
- 10 oz cremini mushrooms, stems discarded, thinly sliced
- 4 cloves garlic, minced
- ¼ cup all-purpose flour
- 1 tsp ground black pepper
- 1 tsp paprika
- 1 Tbsp Worcestershire sauce
- 2 tsp grainy mustard
- 4 cups All the Bones Broth from page 93, or beef or chicken stock
- 8 oz rotini pasta or wide noodle of choice
- ½ cup sour cream
- Dill for garnish

Preheat the oven to 350°F.

Add 2 tablespoons of butter to a Dutch oven over medium-high heat. When the butter melts and begins to brown, add beef and salt and sauté until all of the meat has browned, about 4 to 6 minutes. Remove the beef, set aside, and keep any drippings that collected in the pot.

(Directions continued on next page)

Reduce the heat to medium-low and add 3 additional tablespoons of butter to the pot. When the butter melts and begins to brown, add onion and mushrooms and sauté until the onion is soft and beginning to caramelize, about 12 to 15 minutes. Stir in garlic and sauté for 1 minute. Thoroughly incorporate flour into the onion-mushroom mixture.

Stir in pepper, paprika, Worcestershire sauce, mustard, and the remaining 1 teaspoon of salt and continue to sauté for 2 minutes. Pour in broth or stock and continually stir to break down any clumps. Increase the heat to medium-high and bring to a simmer. Remove from the heat.

Add browned beef, cover with a lid, and transfer to the oven and braise until the meat is tender, about 50 to 60 minutes.

Carefully remove the pot from the oven and the lid from the pot. Stir in pasta, replace the lid, and return to the oven to continue to braise until the pasta is cooked, about 15 to 20 minutes.

Remove the stroganoff from the oven, remove the lid, and stir in sour cream. Or, offer sour cream and dill to guests to garnish their own bowl. *Dosvedanya!*

Chapter 5

NONE OF THE ABOVE

Kālua and Coffee

In this case, we mean Hawaiian pork . . . and coffee!

This one time in China . . . By now you've come to expect an opening like that, huh? Look, a lot of my culinary adventures took place in China, alright? So, like I was saying, this one time in China, Howie and I were planning to cook a traditional Hawaiian luau on the lovely sands of Hainan Island, led by the classic *kalua pork*. Kalua means to cook in an underground pit. The idea was just wacky enough to work, as the Chinese go mad for any permutation of roasted pork and here we were on a tropical island. What could go wrong? *Party!*

As it turned out, plenty could go wrong: A) it started to rain; B) as we dug a hole for the pork, we ran into power cables; C) the continued rain made fire building pretty challenging; D) we ran out of kindling; E) we couldn't find stones big enough to hold the heat in the pit; F) once we covered up the pit and waited, anxiety crept in. Will it cook? We didn't know, but we certainly had 30 mouths to feed in a few hours.

Phew! It all worked out! 1) we did a reverse rain dance; 2) we dug a second hole *far* away; 3) we got a workout from all the fanning of dismal flames; 4) nearby restaurant staff started breaking old wooden chairs to help us out; 5) we used bricks from a building that was just torn down; 6) all that anxiety was for naught. We're just lucky cooks. Kalua pork was a hit, and in describing the word *kalua* to my Chinese friends, Kahlúa coffee-liquor, of which they were aware, kept getting in the way. This gave me an idea. What if kalua pork was made with coffee? Fun, right?

—Greg

TOTAL TIME: 4 hours, 15 minutes | **VESSEL:** 4½ + qt Dutch oven | **SERVES:** 4–6

- 6 oz strong coffee
- 3 tsp liquid smoke
- 1 Tbsp kosher salt
- 4 feet of banana leaves
- 2½–3 lb pork shoulder roast, boneless, well marbled

Preheat the oven to 425°F.

In a small mixing bowl, whisk together coffee, liquid smoke and salt until the salt dissolves.

On a work surface, lay out two feet of aluminum foil in one direction, then 2 more feet at 90 degrees to the first. Then, directly on top of the foil, lay out 2 feet of banana leaf in one direction and 2 more feet at 90 degrees to the first. Place the pork roast atop the center of the banana leaves. The goal here is to surround the pork in a leakproof enclosure, leaving a small opening at the very top.

Carefully pour the coffee mixture into the leaf-foil pouch, then seal up the top with remaining leaf and foil. Place the packet into a Dutch oven and pour

2 cups of water around the pork packet. Place a lid on the pot and transfer to the oven to braise for 4 hours.

Carefully remove the pot from the oven, then the pork packet from the pot. Open the top of the packet and transfer the pork to a mixing bowl, leaving the liquid behind. Use two forks to pull the pork into shred. Use the meat for tacos, sandwiches, atop a bowl of rice, as a topping for pasta, or simply share with a friend and a fork. Aloha!

Why Did the Chicken Cross the Border?

A piquant ode to a Sunday roast

Look, everybody! Another roasted chicken recipe in another Dutch oven cookbook! How unique. It's okay to feel that *Here we go again* feeling before trying this recipe. But, where most roasted chicken recipes stick to the playbook and remain bashful, this application throws away the rules altogether. First, we cover the bird, and essentially steam it for a long time. That's not normal. You see, steaming poultry renders the fat under the skin faster than dry heat. By the time we uncover the pot, the skin is hyper-ready to get crispy/chewy. We also pack the chicken with so much flavor, it will be hard to go back to other boring roast recipes.

—Greg

TOTAL TIME: 2 hours | **VESSEL:** 6–7 qt Dutch oven | **SERVES:** 6–8

- ½ cup, plus 4 Tbsp extra-virgin olive oil, divided
- 4 tsp kosher salt, divided
- ½ tsp ground black pepper
- 1 Tbsp ground cumin
- 1 Tbsp dried oregano
- 2 oz chipotle peppers in adobo
- 4 flour tortillas
- ½ lb beetroot, peeled, sliced into ½-inch rounds
- ½ lb yucca root, peeled, sliced into ½-inch rounds
- 5–6 lb whole chicken, giblets removed
- 1 bunch cilantro, stem-end separated, leaves roughly chopped
- ½ onion, halved
- 2 limes, quartered

Preheat the oven to 400°F.

In a blender or food processor, puree ½ cup olive oil, 2 teaspoons of salt, black pepper, cumin, oregano, and chipotles. Set aside.

Using 1 tablespoon of olive oil, coat the bottom of a Dutch oven. Cover the bottom of the pot with tortillas fanned out atop the oil. Drizzle 1 tablespoon of oil atop the tortillas. Fan out discs of beets and yucca and drizzle with the remaining olive oil and sprinkle with 2 teaspoons of salt.

Pat the chicken dry with paper towels and place atop the beets and yucca, breast-side up. Into the cavity of the chicken, stuff cilantro stems, onion, and lime wedges. Brush the top of the chicken with half of the chipotle puree. Tie the ends of the legs together with kitchen twine.

Place a lid on the pot, transfer to the oven, and roast for 1 hour. Carefully remove the lid and brush the top with the remaining chipotle puree. Continue to roast for 30 to 40 minutes, until the chicken skin is crispy and brown. Remove the pot from the oven. Using sturdy tongs, remove the chicken from the pot and transfer

(Directions continued on next page)

to a rimmed baking sheet. Using a spatula, transfer the beets and yucca to a platter. Remove the tortillas from the bottom of the pot and place in a separate bowl. They will be mush and they ain't pretty, but man, are they delish!

Transfer the chicken to a cutting board and carve into pieces before serving alongside beets and yucca and a bit of the dementedly delectable tortilla sludge. This goes well with Those Beans from That Mexican Place on page 52 and the Oaxacasserole on page 121.

BIGel

Yeah, it's a really big bagel

It's fun and fairly disturbing when social media erupts over something food-dumb. Is the Aperol spritz actually a disgusting cocktail? Does pineapple belong on pizza? Is a hot dog a sandwich? I actually know the answers, but you'll have to wait. Anyhow, people get all bent out of shape over such nonsense, where food should the ultimate uniter, right? My favorite moronic debate came just a little while ago in the form of the great bagel debate. You see, in St. Louis, notably, when serving a crowd, sometimes bagels are cut crosswise instead of sandwich style. Sort of like creating pre-toasted bagel chips.

Well, the fury was fast around this slicing preference and people quickly took sides. How stupid. We all know that bagels should never be cut at all! Kidding. This world-class-idiotic argument over a bagel got me thinking, when *wouldn't* cutting the bagel into spread-worthy slices be potentially offensive? The answer is clear: If the bagel is *gigantic*! As you read through this recipe, you'll note that it's not an everyday affair, and is most likely suitable as a wow-presentation at your next party. It's a concept more than it is a recipe. Still, you should really do it to show off. Oh, and my answers, in order: No, no, and no.

—Howie

TOTAL TIME: 3 hours | **VESSEL:** 5–6 qt Dutch oven, plus an empty, cleaned 28-oz metal can | **SERVES:** 6–8

- 1½ cups plus 1 Tbsp water, divided
- 1 Tbsp kosher salt
- 1 Tbsp brown sugar
- 1 Tbsp rapid-rise or active dry yeast
- 1 lb all-purpose or bread flour, plus more for surface-dusting
- 1 Tbsp extra-virgin olive oil
- ¼ cup honey
- 1 egg white
- 2 Tbsp poppy seeds, or other favorite bagel topping

In a small mixing bowl, whisk together water, salt, and brown sugar until everything dissolves. If you're using active dry yeast, bloom the yeast in the liquid for 5 minutes before adding to the dry ingredients.

In a large mixing bowl or the bowl of a stand mixer, whisk together rapid-rise yeast and flour. With clean hands or on low speed with a dough hook in the stand mixer, slowly incorporate the liquid until a single mass of dough forms. Whether by hand or mixer, knead the dough for 5 minutes.

On a flour-dusted work surface, knead and form the dough into a smooth ball and transfer to a large bowl greased with olive oil. Cover with plastic or a clean towel and allow the dough to ferment for an hour at room temperature. At this time, place a Dutch oven covered with its lid in the oven and preheat to 425°F.

(Directions continued on page 179)

Transfer the dough to a flour-dusted work surface and punch down. Once again, knead the dough into a smooth ball. Dust with additional flour, cover with plastic or a clean towel, and set aside for 30 minutes. Uncover the dough. To form the bagel shape, press a pointer finger into the center of the dough, pushing down to the work surface. Firmly press and move the finger in a spiral shape to widen the hole as it forms. The goal is to get the hole as wide as a 28-oz can. Cover the dough and set aside for 20 minutes.

In a wide-bottomed straight-sided skillet, boil 2 inches of water on high. Stir in the honey. Reduce the heat to medium. Uncover the dough and carefully lower into the simmering liquid, being sure to retain the round shape as much as possible. After 45 seconds, using two spatulas, carefully flip the dough. Simmer for another 45 seconds, then remove the dough ring to a sheet pan.

In a small mixing bowl, whisk together the egg white and 1 tablespoon of water. Brush the top of the dough ring with the egg mixture and sprinkle with a generous amount of poppy seeds. Carefully remove the Dutch oven from the oven and remove the lid. Place the empty can in the center of the pot. Again using two spatulas, carefully transfer the dough ring into the pot, surrounding the can. Transfer the pot back to the oven and bake the BIGel for 45 minutes.

Remove the pot from the oven and remove the lid. Using two spatulas, remove the BIGel from the pot. Allow it to cool for at least 30 minutes before slicing and serving with whatever rings your bell.

Full-Power Cauliflower

A full-headed roasting experience

It can be tough to make white food stand out on the dinner table alongside more colorful fare. Think about it. Mashed potatoes alone, meh. Mashed potatoes with a glossy, dark gravy, brilliant. A glass of milk, meh. A glass of chocolate milk, awesome. Cauliflower suffers and remains uninspired when steamed and boiled. Roasting or sautéing seasoned florets does a lot to add taste, but it is tough to get beyond the boredom of a white vegetable, just sitting there.

So, what to do? How about marinating the cauliflower in a deep red goop, and roasting it whole? And then presenting it, as such, to the table—whole and in all its glory. Perhaps the most fun is that everyone gets to hack away at it with a knife. Dramatic, fun, and flavorful. What a combo!

—Greg

TOTAL TIME: 3 hours | **VESSEL:** 4–6 qt Dutch oven | **SERVES:** 4–6

1 head cauliflower
2/3 cup extra-virgin olive oil
1/3 cup lime juice
1 tsp honey
1 tsp kosher salt
1 tsp ground cumin
1 tsp paprika
1 tsp ground black pepper
1 tsp garlic powder
2 tsp dried oregano

Trim the stem of the cauliflower so that it sits flat and completely within the walls of the Dutch oven. In a mixing bowl that (ideally just) fits the upside-down head of cauliflower, briskly whisk together the remaining ingredients. Place the cauliflower head-down in the mixing bowl so that the marinade makes optimal contact with the cauliflower. Cover with plastic and set aside for 2 hours. Every so often, carefully swirl the bowl around so as to encourage the top of the head of cauliflower to make contact with marinade.

Preheat the oven to 425°F.

Carefully lift the cauliflower out of the marinade and flip over into a Dutch oven. Using a pastry brush, paint the top of the cauliflower with marinade that remains in the mixing bowl. Place the lid on the pot and transfer into the oven to roast for 40 to 50, or until a knife can easily be slid into the flesh of the cauliflower. Carefully remove the lid, turn the oven to broil, and let the cauliflower brown for 5 minutes.

Serve hot on a plate for folks to pick at with a fork and knife.

Open Sesame . . . Eggplant

A magic carpet ride to aubergine-land

Whoever gave eggplant its name was probably not a great maker of eggplant dishes. See, choosing the right eggplant is key to the success of any eggplant dish. And a big purple ovule that resembles an alien egg may be exactly the wrong choice. Howie will disagree with me but read on. *Go, Team Greg!*

The wider the eggplant bulb, the more you'll find seeds. And while eggplant seeds are fantastic for growing eggplants, they are not great for eating. They can be a bit bitter, and the flesh around them is springy and spongy—perfect for soaking up a ton of oil, but devoid of any serious flavor.

My advice is to choose the thinnest eggplant you can find. Heavier for its size is another good sign, as is firm to the touch. Japanese and Chinese eggplants are best, but any relatively thin eggplant will do. Even with the marvels of modern agriculture and transportation, eggplants remain seasonal. If there isn't a good one at your market, just make another dish.

—Greg

TOTAL TIME: 30 min | **VESSEL:** 3 qt Dutch oven | **SERVES:** 3–4, as a side dish

1 tsp vegetable oil
1 Tbsp soy sauce
2 Tbsp roasted sesame oil
½ tsp kosher salt
2–3 Chinese or Japanese eggplants, cut into 1-inch rounds
10 cloves garlic, minced
¼ tsp red pepper flakes (optional)
2 scallions, thinly sliced

Preheat the oven to 400°F.

In a Dutch oven, mix the vegetable oil, soy sauce, roasted sesame oil, and salt. Add the eggplant, garlic, and red pepper flakes, if using and toss to coat. Cover and place the pot in the oven for 20 to 30 minutes, until the eggplant is cooked through.

Remove from the oven and serve over rice with the sliced scallions.

Salmon of the Gods

The secret to fully cooked fish that feels rare

I've always liked my salmon cooked rare all the way through, and I currently adore chewy skin. That's weird, right? I went through a phase during which I was trying to achieve the perfect crispy skin, and I was successful. But, the flesh was medium-rare at best, and obviously well done on the edges. Had to move on. I needed to learn to like chewy skin if I were to reach the ultimate flesh consistency. More than a few visits to the local sushi joint turned out to be quite eye-opening. Salmon skin rolls, nigiri or atop chirashi bowls, I was finally into it. So, I set out to end up with chewy skin and the coveted rare all the way through.

A skillet would be wrong, as you're just asking for uneven cooking through the thickness. So, I wondered, what would happen if we preheat the Dutch oven, just as in a bread recipe, but instead of returning the pot to the oven with the fish inside, we left the salmon to cook in the residual heat of the pot itself? Would it be enough heat to do the job? Will I ever be happy? Tune in below and cook it already.

—Howie

TOTAL TIME: 50 minutes | **VESSEL:** 6+ qt Dutch oven | **SERVES:** 6–8

- 7 Tbsp extra-virgin olive oil, divided
- 1 lemon, juiced
- 1 tsp kosher salt
- ½ tsp ground black pepper
- 1 tsp smoked paprika
- 1 tsp onion powder
- 1 tsp garlic powder
- 2 Tbsp chopped dill
- 2½ lb salmon, single side or fillets

Preheat the oven to 425°F and place a Dutch oven with its lid on into the oven as it heats.

After 30 minutes, in a mixing bowl, whisk together 4 tablespoons of olive oil, lemon juice, salt, pepper, paprika, onion powder, garlic powder, and dill. Brush the flesh side of the salmon with the mixture.

Carefully remove the hot Dutch oven from the oven and remove the lid. Drizzle 3 tablespoons of olive oil onto the bottom of the pot and place the salmon, skin-side down. Place the lid back on the pot and let it sit for 20 minutes.

Remove the lid and serve healthy doses of perfect salmon with literally any starch. It's also a fantastic partner to the Ratatouille from page 81.

Polenta Without the Workout

Forget stir, stir, stir; how about sit, sit, sit?

Please see the introduction for *You Could Have Been Baking Your Risotto* from page 137 and swap out "risotto" for "polenta." You'll understand my uncharacteristic brevity in a moment.

—Greg

TOTAL TIME: 1 hour | **VESSEL:** 3½–5 qt Dutch oven | **SERVES:** 6–8

- 6 cups water
- 1½ cups whole milk
- 1 tsp kosher salt
- ½ tsp black pepper
- 2 cups polenta or coarse cornmeal
- 4 Tbsp butter
- ½ cup Parmesan cheese, grated or shredded, plus more for garnish

Preheat the oven to 375°F.

Add water, milk, salt, pepper, and polenta into unheated Dutch oven and stir to combine.

Transfer the pot to the oven and cook, uncovered, for 50 minutes. Remove the pot from the oven, and vigorously stir the polenta. After stirring for about a minute, clean and wet the spoon to smooth out the surface. Return to the oven, uncovered, for another 10 minutes.

Remove the pot from oven. Stir butter and cheese into polenta, until fully melted and incorporated. Sprinkle with additional grated Parmesan cheese and serve immediately. If you're feeling crazy, top it with Yes, Grandma, We'll Call It Gravy from page 19!

Bread Head

Oh, just read the story

A bread story too good not to recount:

We have a wonderfully entertaining Chinese buddy named Qu Feng, an archaeologist and our go-to guy for historical perspective on Chinese cuisine. A while back, we had a lengthy discussion about food nomenclature, and it all started with the ubiquitous, fluffy white bun called a *mantou*. Mantou, according to Qu Feng, was originally *yemantou*, or "head of the barbarian!" Sounds delicious, no?

The story goes that the famous general and statesman during the Three Kingdoms period, Zhuge Liang, was leading his troops away from battle with many prisoners of war. They came across a raging river that they found improbable to cross. The general came up with a gruesomely simple way to appease the river gods and calm the waters. "What if we decapitated our prisoners and tossed just the heads into the horrendous current," pondered Zhuge Liang. "That's sure to ease the angry flow." Seems a weird gamble, right?

As legend has it, it worked. The only trouble is, eventually they'd reach a mad torrent with not a prisoner in sight. "Let's fool the river gods by replacing the real heads with bread heads, filled with meat, like brains!" Again, it worked, and *mantou* were born! As the Chinese have a tendency toward linguistic gymnastics, filled buns were replaced by the term *baozi* and *mantou* morphed into simple steamed white bread.

Anyhow, our Bread Head is not the bread head of Chinese legend, but it is bread and is the size of a head, so there you have it.

—Greg

TOTAL TIME: 3 hours, 30 minutes | **VESSEL:** 5–6 qt Dutch oven | **SERVES:** 6–8

- 1½ cups water
- 1 Tbsp kosher salt
- 1 Tbsp rapid-rise or active dry yeast
- 1 lb all-purpose or bread flour, plus more for surface-dusting
- 1 Tbsp extra-virgin olive oil

In a small mixing bowl, whisk together water and salt until the salt dissolves. If you're using active dry yeast, bloom the yeast in the liquid for 5 minutes before adding to the dry ingredients.

In a large mixing bowl or the bowl of a stand mixer, whisk together rapid-rise yeast and flour. With clean hands or low speed with a dough hook in the stand-mixer, slowly incorporate the liquid until a single mass of dough forms. Whether by hand or mixer, knead the dough for 5 minutes.

On a flour-dusted work surface, knead and form the dough into a smooth ball and transfer to a large bowl greased with olive oil. Cover with plastic or a clean towel and allow the dough to ferment for 1 hour, 30 minutes at room temperature.

After 1 hour, place a Dutch oven covered with its lid in the oven and preheat to 425°F.

After another 30 minutes, transfer the dough to a flour-dusted work surface and punch down. Once again, knead the dough into a smooth ball. Dust with additional flour, cover with plastic or a clean towel, and set aside for 30 minutes.

Uncover the dough. Carefully remove the Dutch oven from the oven and remove the lid. Carefully transfer the dough ball into the pot. Transfer the pot back to the oven and bake for 45 minutes.

Remove the pot from the oven, and remove the lid. Remove the bread to a cooling rack. Allow it to rest for at least 30 minutes before slicing and serving with whatever rings your bell. If you're feeling creative, freeze the bread for 30 minutes and slice huge rounds for the Cheesy Skyscraper Sandwich on page 191.

Cheesy Skyscraper Sandwich

A.k.a. the hot Dagwood

Have you been to a car show? Those concept cars can be mighty impressive, with their space-age design, booster engines, streamlined curves, AI best friend in the dash, and of course, hyperdrive. Think of this recipe as a *concept dish*. Just as you can't drive off the lot with that concept car you just drooled over at the expo center, you can't just eat this sandwich, it may even prove foolhardy to dare cook it. Well, not in the traditional ways. Here is a crazy thought. What if you just totally ignored this recipe and bounced on over to the next?

WAIT (insert vinyl record screech). I got it. Here is the way to do it. You cook this behemoth of a sandwich—if you can call it that. Then, drive 9 equally spaced wooden skewers down from top to bottom. Then, cut the thing into 9 even awesome kebabs! Oh, and if you understand the reference to Dagwood Bumstead's sandwich preferences—congratulations, we're both old.

—Greg

TOTAL TIME: 50 minutes | **VESSEL:** 4–5 qt Dutch oven | **SERVES:** 4–6

7 pieces sandwich bread
4 oz salami slices
4 oz ham slices
4 oz smoked turkey slices
6 oz American cheese slices
6 oz Colby Jack cheese slices
6 oz provolone cheese slices
2 Tbsp extra-virgin olive oil

Place a Dutch oven with its lid in the oven and preheat to 325°F.

Build a 6-layer sandwich with the meats and cheeses, being sure to include cheese bordering each slice of bread.

After the Dutch oven has been in the preheated oven for 30 minutes, carefully transfer the pot to the counter. Remove the lid and use a pastry brush or paper towel to spread olive oil on the pot bottom and the bottom of the lid. Using oven gloves, carefully lift the 6-decker sandwich and place it at the bottom of the pot.

Place the lid back on top of the pot and press down on the sandwich within. The lid may not want to stay all the way down, and you may need to get creative by placing something heavy and oven-safe atop the lid.

Place the pot back in the oven and roast until the top and bottom slices of bread are nicely browned and the cheese is melted throughout, about 15 to 20 minutes. Remove the pot from the oven and sandwich from the pot.

Slice and serve in any number of creative ways.

Queso FUN-dido

Cheese dip with attitude

(Spoiler alert: I'm about to rant about food words again. You've been warned.)

Can you imagine this scenario? Family sits down at a local diner and asks the server, "may we have a bowl of cheese, please?" No. You can't imagine it, unless this is one seriously quirky family. But, when this same family sits down at a Mexican restaurant and orders "queso," *it is the same exact thing!*

We're not dummies, so why do we call *chile con queso* by the Spanish word for "cheese" and leave out the word that differentiates chile con queso from just *queso*? What's wrong with keeping chile in there? It literally defines the dish! Are we really that lazy, or do we actively hate using proper terminology? What's next, calling a hamburger patty a *burger*, which means a representative on a German town council? Oh, wait, you already do. I'm out of here!

Rant over. Now, please enjoy the cooking and the eating of another one of my favorites, which takes your average chile con queso and makes it special with sausage. It's *queso fundido*, or molten cheese. Arg!

—Howie

TOTAL TIME: 20 minutes | **VESSEL:** 3–5 qt Dutch oven | **SERVES:** 4–6

- 3 Tbsp extra-virgin olive oil, divided
- 10 oz Mexican chorizo sausage, raw, casing removed
- 1 onion, diced
- ½ tsp kosher salt
- 1 (4-oz) can chopped green chiles
- 1 Tbsp all-purpose flour
- 2 cups milk
- 16 oz cheddar cheese, shredded

Add 1 tablespoon of olive oil to a Dutch oven over medium-high heat. When the oil begins to shimmer, add sausage and sauté for 5 to 6 minutes, or until the meat is well browned, breaking it up as it cooks. Using a slotted spoon, remove the sausage to a plate.

Add 2 remaining tablespoons of olive oil to the pot. When the oil begins to simmer, add onion and salt and sauté for 5 to 7 minutes, or until the onion is soft and beginning to brown. Add chiles and flour and continue to sauté for 1 minute. Pour in milk and stir as the mixture comes to a simmer.

When the liquid is visibly thickened, stir in the cooked sausage. Begin adding small handfuls of cheese and stir until each melts into the fundido.

When the last bit of cheese has melted into the fundido, serve immediately with tortilla chips. OR, make ahead and reheat over medium-low until the fundido is once again gooey and bubbly.

Not a Pancake

Well, it is, but it's not

We've all been there. You can't decide between pancakes and pizza. Am I in the mood to fold my food or smother my food with maple syrup? *No, that's the wrong approach. Nobody has those moods.*

Have you ever dreamed of combining your love for pizza and your obsession with pancakes? Now's your chance! Introducing the Dutch oven pan-pizza. *Hold on, that's already a thing. Rewrite.*

This is not a pancake. This is not a pizza. It's a little bit of both but the entirety of neither. *Better. Much, much better.*

—Greg

TOTAL TIME: 30 minutes | **VESSEL:** 3+ qt Dutch oven | **SERVES:** 1–2

3 eggs
½ cup water
2 Tbsp soy sauce
½ cup all-purpose flour
1 tsp kosher salt
½ tsp ground black pepper
4 cloves garlic
4 Tbsp extra-virgin olive oil

Suggested omnivore toppings:

4 oz salami or pepperoni
4 oz shredded cheddar cheese

Suggested vegetarian toppings:

1 red bell pepper, roasted, peeled, seeded, sliced into ¼-inch strips
½ cup black olives, pitted, halved
¾ cup Parmesan cheese, grated

Preheat the oven to 425°F with a Dutch oven inside.

In a blender, puree eggs, water, soy sauce, flour, salt, pepper, and garlic.

Add olive oil to the pot in the oven and continue to heat for 5 minutes.

Carefully remove the heated pot from the oven, pour in batter, and add toppings of choice. Return the pot to the oven to bake until the edges have puffed and browned, about 18 to 20 minutes.

Serve hot, rolled up like a taquito.

For All the Cheese in China

Red-cooked potatoes never saw this coming

Greg and I have a very good friend in China named Dave Fan. A jack of all trades, really. Entrepreneur, travel guide, TV fixer for Bourdain, gourmand, and restaurateur. If you were a Western traveler swinging through Chengdu in the 1990s, you knew of "Dave's Oasis" as the first of the now all-but-gone wandering Bohemian watering holes. Dave's was the place you'd visit if you got as far as Sichuan. It was where you took a load off after a burning desire to run away from the smelly hostel. Most importantly, it was the only place, for a very long time, where you could eat an ingenious fusion of Sichuan cuisine and pizza.

We already knew that China doesn't really do cheese, and you almost never see Chinese dishes paired with it. According to a Chinese archaeologist friend, "we never liked milk. Why would we enjoy old, rotten milk?" *Well, when you put it that way . . .* How did Dave or the magic of Chengdu make it possible for kung pao chicken pizza or mapo tofu pizza to even work? My guess was that the individual elements of the dishes played well with cheese with no pretense of an inherent conflict. So, after truly enjoying Dave's handiwork, we got to some experimenting of our own. Potatoes and cheese, check. Scallions, garlic, and cheese, check. Soy sauce, ginger, and cheese, there was the unknown, the culinary beyond. We had no idea when this all began. It works, and works well.

—Howie

TOTAL TIME: 1 hour, 30 minutes | **VESSEL:** 4½+ qt Dutch oven | **SERVES:** 6–8

- 4 Tbsp extra-virgin olive oil, divided
- 5–6 Yukon gold potatoes
- 1 tsp kosher salt
- 6 cloves garlic, minced
- 1 inch ginger, minced
- 3 Tbsp Shaoxing or other Chinese rice wine, or dry sherry
- 2 Tbsp soy sauce
- 2 Tbsp mushroom or other dark soy sauce
- 1 tsp Chinese black vinegar or balsamic vinegar
- 4 scallions, white and green parts separated, thinly sliced
- 6 oz cheddar cheese, shredded
- Sour cream for garnish

Grease the inside of a Dutch oven using 1 tablespoon of olive oil. Poke the potatoes several times with a fork. Place the potatoes on the bottom of the pot and close with a lid. Transfer the pot to the oven and preheat to 375°F. From the moment that the oven is fully heated, continue to roast the potatoes for 30 minutes.

Carefully remove the pot from the oven and the lid from the pot. Using tongs, turn the potatoes over, replace the lid, and return the pot to the oven to continue roasting for 30 minutes.

Remove the pot from the oven and the lid from the pot. Leaving the potatoes in place, carefully slice their tops open lengthwise. Using a potato masher, squash the potatoes to an even height of about 1½ inches.

(Directions continued on next page)

In a mixing bowl, whisk together salt, garlic, ginger, wine or sherry, soy sauces, and vinegar. Evenly pour the mixture across the top of the potatoes. Top with remaining olive oil, scallion whites, and cheese. Return the pot to the oven until the cheese melts and begins to look toasty for 15 minutes. Remove the very confused potatoes from the oven, garnish with remaining scallions, and serve hot scoops as a side with sour cream for topping.

Grilled Cheese, Reimagined

One gooey pull-apart bread

Grilled cheese should be a group affair. Look, we all love a great toasty, gooey grilled cheese. Why not take it away from the individual eats column and force-feed it to the party category? No, of course nobody has ever asked for this, but did we ask for 3-D television? No. Did we request the invention of the countertop deep fryer? No. Did we beg for the cross-bred tiger/lion, the Liger? Look at how popular those things are today! Group Grilled Cheese is sure to be a hit!

More seriously, however, we thought about this long and hard and found inspiration in monkey bread. It's a delicious dessert that sometimes masquerades as an appetizer. Think everything you love about a cinnamon roll but in a mountain of pull-apart bread nuggets. Replace all that brown sugar cinnamon deliciousness with stretchy cheese and punchy green onions. I look forward to the day where sitting by your lonesome enjoying the native entertainment of melty goodness is obsolete. Long live communal munchies! And Ligers!

—Howie

TOTAL TIME: 3 hours | **VESSEL:** 5–6 qt Dutch oven | **SERVES:** 6–8

- 1½ cups water
- 1 Tbsp kosher salt
- 1 Tbsp rapid-rise or active dry yeast
- 1 lb all-purpose or bread flour, plus more for surface-dusting
- 3 Tbsp extra-virgin olive oil, divided
- 1 tsp garlic powder
- 3 scallions, green parts, thinly sliced
- 10 oz cheese, shredded

In a small mixing bowl, whisk together water and salt until the salt dissolves. If you're using active dry yeast, bloom the yeast in the liquid for 5 minutes before adding to the dry ingredients.

In a large mixing bowl or the bowl of a stand mixer, whisk together rapid-rise yeast and flour. With clean hands or low speed with a dough hook in the stand mixer, slowly incorporate the liquid until a single mass of dough forms. Whether by hand or mixer, knead the dough for 5 minutes.

On a flour-dusted work surface, knead and form the dough into a smooth ball and transfer to a large bowl greased with olive oil. Cover with plastic or a clean towel and allow the dough to ferment for 1 hour, 30 minutes at room temperature.

After 1 hour, place a Dutch oven covered with its lid in the oven and preheat to 425°F.

(Directions continued on page 201)

After 1 hour, 30 minutes, transfer the dough to a flour-dusted work surface and punch down. Roll the dough out to a ¼-inch approximate rectangle. Drizzle half of the surface of the dough with remaining 2 tablespoons of olive oil. Sprinkle the same half with garlic powder, scallions, and cheese. Fold the uncovered half of the dough over the top of the covered half of the dough and press down firmly.

Using a knife or pizza cutter, cut the filled dough into smaller rectangles about 2 x 2 square-inch. Pick up one filled dough segment and press it into a ball in the palm of one hand. Set aside on a flour-dusted sheet pan and repeat with the remaining dough segments. Cover the lot with plastic and allow them to rest for 15 minutes.

Remove the Dutch oven from the oven and carefully remove the lid. Place a layer of dough balls at the bottom of the pot and continue to place them in a cone shape toward a single peak. Replace the lid of the pot and return it to the oven and bake for 45 minutes. Remove the lid and continue to bake until the top surfaces are golden brown, about 15 to 20 minutes.

Remove the bread concoction from the oven and serve to eager, hungry, interested folk to pull apart at will!

The Grape Leaves of Wrath

Just a fun title, stuffed grape leaves are kind

I've made a few mistakes in my life. That woman in college I dated even though everyone told me she was horrible. Falling madly in love with a woman who lived 3,000 miles away. Deciding to show off my eggplant-slicing skills on a first date and ending up with a bloody thumb and not even a courtesy second date. Anyone sensing a pattern?

Well, perhaps the biggest mistake is something I've been dumb enough to do twice: Convincing a date to try a stuffed grape leaf. I mean, life before that was great. We'd order the combo veggie appetizer plate, and I'd get both of the grape leaves. What could be better? But some twisted thing inside of me insisted on trying to share my love of this food. And each time, the first bite sealed my fate.

The first time I tried this, she took one bite, excused herself, and never came back. Sometimes I try to convince myself that she just couldn't handle how awesome my palate was and ran for the hills. The second time I was generous with the grape leaves, but the story couldn't have been more different and ended with an ironic twist. She took one bite, then another, then took the other one off the plate. I was very confused. This simple action confirmed that she was the love of my life, but I would also be sentenced to competing for grape leaves forever!

I found a solution. Forget about the appetizer plate at the Greek place. Make a big pot of grape leaves yourself. Enough to share! (Or wait until she leaves town for the weekend and keep them all for yourself!)

—Greg

TOTAL TIME: 30 minutes | **VESSEL:** 6 qt Dutch oven | **SERVES:** 8–10

- 2 pounds ground beef
- 1 cup long-grain white rice, uncooked
- 2 tomatoes, chopped finely
- 1½ tsp salt
- ¼ tsp pepper
- ½ tsp cinnamon
- 1 jar brined grape leaves, with their liquid
- Juice of 2 lemons

In a mixing bowl, thoroughly combine the beef, rice, tomatoes, salt, pepper, and cinnamon.

In a separate bowl, pour the grape leaves and brine out of the jar. Find a few ugly, torn, or otherwise non-stuffable leaves. Use 6 to 8 of these to completely line the bottom of a Dutch oven.

Now find a pretty leaf. With scissors, cut a ¼-inch "V" around the stem to remove it and the thick vein. Lay the leaf down, veiny-side up, and place about 1 tablespoon of meat mixture in the center of it. Fold the bottom of the leaf (where you cut the stem) up to just cover the meat, then fold in the left side, then the right. Now, loosely roll toward the top of the leaf, making a little burrito. Make sure to keep it a bit loose so that it doesn't burst when the rice cooks and plumps up.

(Directions continued on next page)

As you finish one leaf package, place it, seam-side down, in the Dutch oven. Repeat again and again, layering the packages on top of each other, until you've run out of meat mixture. Cover the tower of stuffed leaves with 6 to 10 empty leaves, like you used at the bottom of the pot.

Gently pour in enough water to cover the stuffed leaves, about 4 cups. Add the lemon juice and ¼ cup of the brine from the grape leaf jar. Place an empty plate on top of the leaves to weigh them down.

Place the Dutch oven on the stovetop over medium heat. Bring to a light boil then turn down the heat to a very light simmer. Cover the Dutch oven and allow it to simmer for 20 to 25 minutes.

I'm told that the stuffed leaves are best served at room temperature, but I've never let them sit around for long enough to tell.

Not Your Grandma's Cabbage Rolls

Because they are *my* grandma's cabbage rolls

My grandmother was an amazing woman. She ran away from home at age 13, created a new name for herself, found her way to the United States, and settled in Chicago where she and a couple sisters found jobs and managed to thrive. Years later, she took a train to California for a visit, decided she was done with winter for the rest of her life, and never left. *Thanks, Grandma!*

Yes, my grandmother was an amazing woman. But she was not an exciting cook. Every recipe was the same. Fry an onion. Add ketchup. Add some meat. Serve. I fear that, if the world were full of Grandma Thebes, there wouldn't be much of a market for cookbooks. And if there were no cookbooks, she never could have bragged about her grandson, the bestselling author. The tragedy!

The crazy part about all this is that her food tasted really good. I mean, I'm sure I'd get tired of it pretty quickly, but ketchup and meat, while it sounds bland, is sweet and sour and savory and salty, all at once. Don't believe me? Give my grandma's cabbage rolls a try. And, if you cleaned your plate, she'd even give you a piece of "the good stuff"—a bite from her stash of dark chocolate.

—Greg

FOR THE CABBAGE ROLLS:

1 head green cabbage, hard core removed

2 pounds ground beef

1 cup uncooked white rice

2 tomatoes, chopped finely

1½ tsp salt

¼ tsp pepper

FOR THE SAUCE:

2 tsp oil

2 onions, chopped

28 oz can pureed tomatoes

½ cup ketchup

¼ cup brown sugar

¼ cup raisins

1 tsp salt

¼ tsp pepper

Juice of 2 lemons

Bring a large pot of salted water to boil—enough to cover or nearly cover your whole cabbage. Using tongs, place the whole cored cabbage in the boiling water. After about 5 minutes, the outermost leaves will begin to separate from the head. Gently pull them off with the tongs, and reserve them to in colander. Repeat with each leaf, until you get to the small guys at the center that are too small to stuff. Discard the water and these last tiny leaves.

Preheat the oven to 350°F. Make the sauce by heating oil in a skillet or Dutch oven over medium-high heat. When the oil begins to shimmer, add the onions, and sauté for 4 to 5 minutes, until the onions are soft and a bit clear. Add the tomatoes, ketchup, brown sugar, raisins, salt, pepper, and lemon juice. Bring to a boil, and lower the heat to a low simmer. Cover and allow to cook for 15 minutes, while you stuff the cabbage.

In a bowl, mix the beef, rice, chopped tomatoes, salt, and pepper. Lay out one cabbage leaf and place about ¼ cup of beef mixture on the bottom-center of the leaf.

(Directions continued on page 207)

(Smaller leaves will be less, larger leaves more. You'll get a feel for it.) Fold from the bottom to the top to just cover the meat. Then fold in each side and roll it over. Don't roll it too tightly, as the rice will expand a bit. Place the roll seam-side down in a Dutch oven, leaving a bit of room between rolls for the sauce to pour into. Repeat until you are out of leaves or filling.

Pour the sauce over the cabbage rolls. Cover and place in the oven for 90 minutes. Remove the cover and bake an additional 30 minutes.

Enjoy warm or hot. Great reheated the next day, as well!

The Pot Lid Can Do That?

Olive oil biscuits in a most convenient place

You didn't know it, but you've been waiting patiently for this moment since you received this book. Finally, this deep into the pages, I will enumerate the vast benefits of cooking in a Dutch oven: 1) They can be used for most methods of cooking from frying and stewing to braising and baking; 2) They come in pretty colors; 3) They can be used as doorstops (watch your toes!); 4) They evenly heat and when covered, the lid maintains the same temperature as the rest of the pot. To boot, if the lid has a smooth underside, guess what? Flip the lid and you got one-pot cooking using two completely different cooking methods!

Something you truly did not know you needed in your life, but all of a sudden, here it is (horns blow and streamers fly). Okay, stop applauding. The only methods the lid will be good for is baking and roasting while you are otherwise making a soup, stew, jam, braise, or casserole. Still, that's pretty snazzy and unexpected. Dazzle your friends with your smarts. When you retrieve the pot from the oven and come to the table with rolls up top and soup down below, you'll surely be voted most likely to make that again for the next party.

The next three recipes are only the start to what can become a habit in your kitchen. I believe it is only one's imagination that can limit what is possible with the Dutch oven lid. By this, I mean absolutely nothing. I think we pretty much covered it all here.

—Howie

TOTAL TIME: 35 minutes | **VESSEL:** Dutch oven lid | **SERVES:** 4–6

- 2½ cup flour, plus more for dusting
- ½ tsp baking soda
- 1 Tbsp baking powder
- ½ tsp salt
- 1 tsp sugar
- ⅓ cup Greek yogurt
- ⅓ cup, plus 3 Tbsp extra-virgin olive oil, divided
- 1 cup milk

NOTE: This recipe presumes that you are already cooking another recipe from this book in the body of the Dutch oven that you will finish in the oven with the lid on. It also presumes the oven temperature is set to 375°F.

In a large mixing bowl, whisk together the flour, baking soda, baking powder, salt, and sugar. In a separate mixing bowl, whisk together the yogurt, olive oil, and milk. Pour the wet ingredients into the dry and mix well until a slightly wet, shaggy dough forms.

Dust a work surface with flour, and transfer the dough from the bowl. Dust the top of the dough with more flour and begin to flatten and mold together with a floured hand and/or a rolling pin. Work the dough until it is ¾-inch thick.

25 minutes before your main recipe is set to be done cooking, place the Dutch oven lid securely upside down on a work surface.

Grease the underside of the lid with 1 tablespoon of olive oil. Cut out dough rounds with a 3-inch biscuit cutter or the top of a 3-inch wide glass. Place the dough rounds on top of the flipped lid, butting up against each other to fit as many as possible. Place the remainder on a greased sheet pan. Drizzle the remaining 2 tablespoons of olive oil over the biscuit dough.

Transfer the otherwise filled Dutch oven with the lid on upside down to the oven and bake until biscuits are starting to brown, about 20 to 25 minutes. Remove the pot from the oven and serve the biscuits with the genius contents of the Dutch oven.

The Pot Lid Can Do That, too?

Roasted potatoes while you wait

TOTAL TIME: 55 minutes | **VESSEL:** Dutch oven lid | **SERVES:** 4–6

1 lb new potatoes, halved, or large potatoes, cut into 1-inch pieces
3 Tbsp extra-virgin olive oil
2 tsp kosher salt
1 tsp ground black pepper
2 tsp ground cumin
1 Tbsp dried oregano

NOTE: This recipe presumes that you are already cooking another recipe from this book in the body of the Dutch oven that you will finish in the oven with the lid on. It also presumes the oven temperature is set to 375°F.

In a large mixing bowl, combine all ingredients.

50 minutes before your main recipe is set to be done cooking, place the Dutch oven lid securely upside down on a work surface. Transfer the seasoned potatoes onto the lid.

Transfer the otherwise filled Dutch oven with the lid on upside down to the oven and bake until the potatoes are golden brown, about 45 to 50 minutes. Remove the pot from the oven and serve the potatoes with the incredible main dish!

This Pot Lid Thing's Getting Ridiculous

Savory and ridiculous dinner rolls

TOTAL TIME: 1 hour, 45 minutes | **VESSEL:** 5–6 qt Dutch oven lid | **SERVES:** 6–8

- 1½ cups water
- 1 Tbsp kosher salt
- 1 Tbsp granulated sugar
- 1 Tbsp rapid-rise or active dry yeast
- 1 lb all-purpose or bread flour, plus more for surface-dusting
- 1 Tbsp extra-virgin olive oil

SUGGESTED OPTIONAL TOPPINGS:

- 2 Tbsp butter, melted with 2 cloves minced garlic
- 2 Tbsp butter, melted with ¼ cup mixed fresh herbs
- 2 Tbsp butter, melted with 2 Tbsp sesame or poppy seeds

NOTE: This recipe presumes that you are already cooking another recipe from this book in the body of the Dutch oven that you will finish in the oven with the lid on. It also presumes the oven temperature will be 375°F.

In a small mixing bowl, whisk together water, salt, and sugar until the salt and sugar dissolve. If you're using active dry yeast, bloom the yeast in the liquid for 5 minutes before adding to the dry ingredients.

In a large mixing bowl or the bowl of a stand mixer, whisk together rapid-rise yeast and flour. With clean hands or low speed with a dough hook in the stand mixer, slowly incorporate the liquid until a single mass of dough forms. Whether by hand or mixer, knead the dough for 5 minutes.

On a flour-dusted work surface, knead and form the dough into a smooth ball and transfer to a large bowl greased with olive oil. Cover with plastic or a clean towel and allow the dough to ferment for an hour at room temperature.

Transfer the dough to a flour-dusted work surface and punch down. Roll the dough into an even snake and cut into 12 equal portions. Roll each portion into a ball, dust with flour, cover with plastic, and set aside for 15 minutes or until ready to use with a companion recipe.

Grease the underside of the Dutch oven lid with olive oil. Line the edge then the middle with dough balls and brush with optional toppings. The dough balls should cover the surface of the underside of the lid. Place the upside-down lid atop the Dutch oven.

Transfer the otherwise filled pot to the oven and bake until the rolls are starting to brown, about 25 to 30 minutes. Remove the pot from the oven, carefully remove the bread-covered lid, and serve the pull-apart bread with whatever awesomeness lives beneath the lid.

Peter Piper Picked a Peck of Stuffed Peppers

More veg, more flavor!

I'm not a fan of traditional stuffed peppers. I mean, they're okay, but a bit boring. This preparation cuts back on the beef, replacing it with more vegetables, and spicing it with the same blend of cinnamon, allspice, and paprika that I use for moussaka or any number of my Greek beef dishes. This is really a "whatever is in your fridge" recipe. Eggplant, zucchini, potatoes, cauliflower, green beans, broccoli—I've even used kohlrabi, it's all good.

Make sure to use wide-bottomed peppers that have plenty of room to hold stuffing and won't fall over in the Dutch oven.

—Greg

TOTAL TIME: 90 min | **VESSEL:** 6 qt Dutch oven | **SERVES:** 4–6

- 6 red or orange bell peppers
- 1 Tbsp oil
- 1 onion, diced
- 4 cloves garlic, roughly chopped
- 1 eggplant, diced
- 1 cauliflower, small florets
- 1 lb ground beef
- ¼ cup pine nuts
- 1 Tbsp tomato paste
- 2 tsp cinnamon
- 2 tsp paprika
- 1 tsp allspice
- 2 tsp kosher salt
- 1 (8-oz) can tomato sauce

Preheat the oven to 400°F

Slice the tops off the peppers. Remove and discard the stems, chopping up the remaining tops. Using a metal spoon, scrape the white ribs and seeds from the peppers.

Place the oil in a Dutch oven over medium-high heat. When the oil begins to shimmer, add the onion. Sauté for 6 to 8 minutes or until it is soft. Add garlic, eggplant, reserved chopped pepper tops, and cauliflower, and continue to sauté until the eggplant starts to brown, about 6 to 8 minutes. Add beef and continue to sauté for 3 to 5 minutes. Add pine nuts, tomato paste, cinnamon, paprika, allspice, and salt. Stir to coat evenly and fry until fragrant, about 2 minutes. Remove mixture from the Dutch oven.

Stuff the 6 peppers with the beef mixture and place them in the Dutch oven. Pour the tomato sauce over the peppers and into the bottom of the pan. Cover and place in the oven for 50 minutes.

Remove from the oven and serve hot.

Big Ole' Pot o' Mussels

And plenty of juicy goodness for bread dippin'

On Friday nights when I was a kid, the scene was usually the same: An order from Vinnie's for pick-up. Large cheese pizza. Yeah, I grew up at the Jersey Shore. You're jealous. We also always had a small tray of sautéed mushrooms and a big tray of mussels simmered in garlicky tomato sauce, which came with a crusty Italian bread loaf. I consistently stayed away from it, as I was not a seafood kid and mussels were just creepy. Creaking open a shiny black shell, oh please! But, I knew they were something special, as the tray was cleared very quickly. As it turns out, I'm glad I grew out of it, because simmered mussels may well be the perfect dish.

Unless you have seafood sensitivities, I urge you to make these on the regular. Changing up the broth is easy enough to do to keep the adventure alive. On nutrition, mussels are a home run: low calorie, low fat, high protein, high omega 3 fatty acids. Then we get to the broth—perhaps the best part. Seafood stock in general has a ton of umami goodness, but there is just something uniquely effective about mussel shells swimming in hot liquid that sets it apart. Going in for huge dips with crusty bread can get addictive. But, if you find yourself moving the mussels aside just for the broth, slow down, buddy. It's a package deal (but save a bowl of just broth for later!)

—Howie

TOTAL TIME: 25 minutes | **VESSEL:** 3+qt Dutch oven | **SERVES:** 2–3

- ¼ cup extra-virgin olive oil
- 5 scallions, white and green parts separated, thinly sliced
- 5 cloves garlic, minced
- 2 (13.5-oz) cans coconut milk
- 1 tsp kosher salt
- ½ tsp ground black pepper
- 1 tsp ground cumin
- 1 tsp ground turmeric
- 1½–2 lb mussels, cleaned, beards removed (discard any that are open)

Add oil to a Dutch oven over medium-high heat. When the oil begins to shimmer, add scallion whites and garlic and sauté until soft, about 3 to 4 minutes. Stir in coconut milk, salt, pepper, cumin, and turmeric, and bring to a boil. Reduce the heat to low and simmer for 10 minutes.

Stir in mussels, place a lid on the pot and simmer until the mussels have all opened up, 7 to 9 minutes.

Remove from the heat and serve right from the pot with Bread Head from page 188, another crusty character. Trust us, this broth is more than sop-worthy!

Roasted Pumpkin Dip

Halloween never tasted so good

This North African dish is certainly something to try once. And once you try it, you probably won't be able to give it up. If your primary frame of reference for pumpkin is its eponymous pie, you are way off. This dish is much closer in taste to the garlic and lemon of hummus. But with the sweet creaminess of squash in the background. Give it a try. You'll never look at a jack-o'-lantern the same way again.

—Greg

TOTAL TIME: 30 minutes | **VESSEL:** 3 qt Dutch oven | **SERVES:** 8–10, as an appetizer

3 Tbsp olive oil
1 onion, chopped
8 cloves garlic, minced or pressed
Small (2 pound) pumpkin, peeled, seeded, and chopped (about 6 cups)
2 tsp cumin
1 tsp paprika
1 tsp curry powder
1 tsp salt
1 tomato, chopped
1 jalapeño, seeded and minced
Juice of 1 lemon

Heat olive oil in a Dutch oven over medium heat. When the oil begins to shimmer, add the onion and sauté for 4 to 5 minutes, until it is soft and a bit clear. Add the garlic and continue to sauté for about 30 seconds, or until fragrant.

Stir in the pumpkin. Cover and allow to cook for 10 minutes.

Uncover the pot and push the pumpkin and onion to the sides, opening up a well in the middle. Drop the cumin, paprika, curry powder, and salt into the center. Let it cook until fragrant, about 20 to 30 seconds. Then, add the tomato and jalapeño, and stir to combine. Cover again and allow to cook for another 10 minutes, or until the pumpkin is fully cooked—it should be soft and falling apart at the edges, but not completely pureed.

Turn off the heat and mash the mixture with a potato masher or the back of a spoon. You are looking for a texture that is mostly smooth, with a few delicious soft chunks. Add the lemon, and extra salt to taste.

Allow the pumpkin dip to cool for an hour or two. Serve at room temperature with pita, crackers, or crispy vegetables.

Overnight Oatmeal to Die for

Though the excitement will likely keep you alive

It's not even fair that this is a recipe in a cookbook. Really, it's a page of advocacy for eating more oatmeal. I, like you, started out as an oatmeal critic. It was either too gummy, gloppy, gooey, or just plain gah! But, once I started to use steel-cut oats and an overnight method of cooking them, the world opened up.

Overnight oats are very simple to make, and the use of steel-cut oats instead of rolled is a genius move. This experience is much like dining on a base of barley, brown rice, farro, or that somehow popular quinoa. The grains of the oats retain some character, a nutty appeal, and you use the method below, re-warmed, they swim in a creamy broth of their own overnight making. The oats give up just enough of their starch to lose any possible gumminess but give a silky texture to the liquids lucky enough to have shared the night. Man, I should be a health food guru.

—Greg

TOTAL TIME: 8 hours, 10 minutes | **VESSEL:** 3–4½ qt Dutch oven | **SERVES:** 8–10

1 Tbsp extra-virgin olive oil
2 cups steel-cut oats (not instant)
¾ tsp salt
3 cups water
1 cup cow, soy, or nut milk

Add oil to a Dutch oven over medium heat. When the oil begins to shimmer, add the oats and salt and sauté until a nutty aroma is apparent, about 1 to 2 minutes.

Add remaining ingredients to the pot over medium-high heat and bring to a boil, stirring to ensure that the oats do not clump. Remove from the heat and place a lid on the pot.

In the morning, if you prefer warm oatmeal, place the pot over low heat and periodically check for the perfect temperature. If you're stocking up on oatmeal for the week, heat up personal amounts in the microwave or in a smaller pot.

Regarding toppings, we have our favorites, though of course, the sky's the limit with oats as a nutty base. Fresh or dry fruits, nuts, yogurt, seeds with funny names, it's all fair game!

Greg's bowl: pomegranate seeds, honey, hazelnuts, and crispy O's cereal
Howie's bowl: chunky peanut butter, sea salt, and extra-virgin olive oil

Chapter 6
DESSERTS

Brownie Mine

A textural adventure awaits!

At first glance, this title is an ode to that 80s alien movie with Dennis Quaid and Louis Gossett Jr., *Enemy Mine*. That would be a really weird reference for a brownie recipe. Unless . . . an Earthling starship pilot gets stranded on another planet only to discover that his sworn enemy, a fudge brownie, is also stranded. Will he eat this antagonist dessert? Will they attempt to survive together and form a lasting bond between human and brownie-kind? Nope. Instead, this title is a suggested game to play with your brownies. It's a group affair. Grab your closest seven friends, some spoons, and scoops of ice cream, and go *mining* for brownie goodness!

Cooking a brownie in a Dutch oven is an adventure you don't often see with brownies. The way the cold pot heats in the oven causes the outer edges of the brownie to crisp up, the bottom to get chewy, the top a tad crusty, and the middle to enjoy layers of varying gooeyness. Much more than your run-of-the-mill brownie. But, this isn't a mill, it's a mine! Who will strike brownie gold first?

—Howie

TOTAL TIME: 1 hour, 15 minutes | **VESSEL:** 3 qt Dutch oven | **SERVES:** 6–8

- 4 eggs
- 2 cups granulated sugar
- ¾ cup butter, melted, plus additional to grease the pot
- ¼ cup chunky peanut butter
- 1 tsp vanilla extract
- ½ tsp kosher salt
- 1 cup all-purpose flour
- ¾ cup cocoa powder

Preheat the oven to 300°F.

In a large mixing bowl, whisk together eggs, sugar, butter, peanut butter, vanilla, and salt until smooth. Stir in flour and cocoa powder until neither is visible.

Grease the insides of a Dutch oven and pour in the batter. Smooth the top and transfer to the oven. Bake until the center of the batter is no longer jiggly, about 45 to 55 minutes. Remove the brownie from the oven and set aside to cool for at least 20 minutes.

Serve a communal crowd in a fun way by topping the brownie with multiple scoops of ice cream and lots of spoons. Alternatively, you can loosen the edges with a spatula and remove the brownie from the Dutch oven and serve warm, gooey slices.

The *This Shouldn't Work* Bread

Chocolate and Gruyère are delicious together

I've seen same-dish chocolate-and-cheese pairings that seemed interesting. Chocolate and Brie grilled cheese chief among them. This sort of thing can be faddish in the same way a social media debate pops up over whether this combination is an abomination or actually works. Many people have their say, then it fades. Does that mean the debate goes away, that opinions have been swayed, or just another social blip on the screen to keep people scrolling and not paying attention to their kids? Just wondering.

I'm also wondering whether this little idea that I dreamed about one fitful night was the result of twisted brain chemistry or true genius. Could it start debates? Wars? Dare I mix chocolate and cheese such that they do not retain their own identity, but instead meld together into a third thing altogether? When I woke up the next morning, if you could call it waking up, I got right to work to see if this was just my brain toying with me or if I crossed into some new culinary territory. Maybe semisweet chocolate for its subtle smoothness and Gruyère cheese for its nuttiness? It couldn't work. Could it?

It worked. It not only worked, it worked so well that I could not decide whether this belonged in the dessert chapter. You decide while I pat myself on the back and make another loaf.

—Howie

TOTAL TIME: 3 hours, 30 minutes | **VESSEL:** 3+ qt Dutch oven | **SERVES:** 6–8

- 2 Tbsp butter, melted
- 1½ cups milk
- 2 tsp kosher salt
- 1 Tbsp granulated sugar
- 1 Tbsp rapid-rise or active dry yeast
- 3 cups all-purpose or bread flour, plus more for surface-dusting
- 1 Tbsp extra-virgin olive oil
- 10 oz semisweet chocolate chips
- 10 oz Gruyère cheese, shredded

In a small mixing bowl, whisk together butter, milk, salt, and sugar until the salt and sugar dissolve. If you're using active dry yeast, bloom the yeast in the liquid for 5 minutes before adding to the dry ingredients.

In a large mixing bowl or the bowl of a stand mixer, whisk together rapid-rise yeast and flour. With clean hands or low speed with a dough hook in the stand mixer, slowly incorporate the liquid until a single mass of dough forms. Whether by hand or mixer, knead the dough for 5 minutes.

On a flour-dusted work surface, knead and form the dough into a smooth ball and transfer to a large bowl greased with olive oil. Cover with plastic or a clean towel and allow the dough to ferment for 1 hour, 30 minutes at room temperature.

(Directions continued on next page)

After 1 hour, place a Dutch oven covered with its lid in the oven and preheat to 425°F.

After another 30 minutes, transfer the dough to a flour-dusted work surface and punch down. Use a rolling pin to form a large 1/8-inch thick rectangle. Distribute chocolate chips and Gruyère across the surface of the dough.

Starting at one edge, roll the dough forward onto itself, enveloping the filling into a tight dough tube. Then, starting at one end of the tube, coil the filled dough into a tight spiral. Once you reach the other end, fold the tip underneath the spiral of dough. Dust with flour, cover with plastic, and set aside for 30 minutes.

Carefully remove the pot from the oven. Uncover the dough round and place in the hot pot. Place the lid on the pot and transfer back to the oven and bake for 35 minutes.

Remove the pot from the oven, and remove the lid. Transfer the bread to a cooling rack. Allow it to rest for at least 30 minutes before slicing and being amazed at what chocolate and cheese do for one another.

Definitely Not a Cinnamon Roll

Oh, but just you wait

Cinnamon rolls are pretty and can be delicious. But, do they have to be impossible to eat without getting completely messy? I'm a neat eater, always have been. For finger foods, I prefer a starchy wrapper. No sticky fingers. For fork and spoon foods, I like sensible cut-ability or orderly scoops. The cinnamon roll has none of this, and you're typically left with two options: 1) Get downright sloppy, then I suppose shower? Or 2) Go at it with a fork and yield unwieldy straps of goop and dough, then I suppose shower?

I sound like a freak, but hear me out. I too love the flavors of a good cinnamon roll, so I set out to get all of the goodness without any of the mess. I started with the premise that the final piece should be forkable and the cinnamon goop had to be there. Did it have to be gooey? Not necessarily, but it had to play a major role. The dough layers were unimportant to me and frankly it would be better as a solid mass. I took a calculated risk, placed wedges of dough, for easy pull-apart action, at the bottom of a pot, and poured the cinnamon sugar goop over the top, coating it and leaving the rest to fall underneath the dough.

It worked so well. Even though the top looked gorgeous with the deeply browned, chewy, puffed-up wedges looked all architectural, I opted to flip the cinnamon monster out of the Dutch oven, exposing the predictably gooey bottom. Replace your typical white icing with vanilla ice cream and *bam*! Finally, I can join team cinnamon roll, just change the team name.

—Howie

TOTAL TIME: 4 hours | **VESSEL:** 4½ qt Dutch oven | **SERVES:** 8–10

FOR THE DOUGH:

1¼ cup milk of choice
2 large eggs
⅓ cup extra-virgin olive oil, plus more for greasing
⅓ cup granulated sugar
1 tsp kosher salt
1 Tbsp rapid-rise or active dry yeast
3½ cups all-purpose flour, plus more for dusting

FOR THE GOOP:

1 cup dark brown sugar, packed
½ tsp kosher salt
2 Tbsp cinnamon
½ cup melted butter

In a small mixing bowl, whisk together milk, eggs, olive oil, sugar, and salt until the salt and sugar dissolve. If you're using active dry yeast, bloom the yeast in the liquid for 5 minutes before adding to the dry ingredients.

In a large mixing bowl or the bowl of a stand mixer, whisk together rapid-rise yeast, if using, and flour. With clean hands or low speed with a dough hook in the stand mixer, slowly incorporate the liquid until a consistent, tacky mass of dough forms. Whether by hand or mixer, knead the dough for 5 minutes.

On a well-flour-dusted work surface, knead and form the dough into a smooth ball and transfer to a large bowl greased with olive oil. Cover with plastic and allow the dough to ferment for 2 hours at room temperature.

(Directions continued on page 231)

Take a nap.

Retaining the round shape, transfer the dough ball to a flour-dusted work surface and dust the top with flour. Evenly press down into a ¾-inch disc. Using a pizza cutter or a long knife, cut the disc into 16 wedges, as best you can, leaving the wedges in the disc shape. Grease the insides of a Dutch oven with a thin coating of olive oil. Using a spatula, a cleaver, or deft hands, transfer the wedges to cover the bottom of the pot.

Preheat the oven to 375°F.

In a microwave-safe bowl, combine brown sugar, salt, cinnamon, and melted butter. Heat the mixture in the microwave for 30 to 40 seconds, or until the sugar and salt have dissolved. Pour the goop around the edges and across the top of the dough wedges, leaving no dough un-gooped. Place a lid on the pot and allow it to rest at room temperature for 1 hour.

Transfer the pot to the oven and bake until the top is well-browned and a bit crackly, about 40 to 50 minutes. Remove the *Definitely Not a Cinnamon Roll* from the oven, and allow it to rest for 10 to 20 minutes.

Place a plate large enough to fit the Dutch oven, or a flat board over the top of the pot. With a firm grip on both the plate/board and the pot handles, carefully flip the pot so that the plate/board sits below. Place the duo down on a work surface and gently lift the pot away from the masterpiece.

Cut hot wedges and serve with vanilla ice cream . . . if you want to be cool.

Molten Blueberries, Anyone?

That's right, serve this coffee cake immediately

When we wrote *One Pan to Rule Them All*, an ode to the cast-iron skillet, I penned the following about coffee cake:

Did it take you as long as it took me to realize that coffee cake was not a cake with coffee in it, but rather something to be served with coffee? As a kid, of course I thought the former, so when I was served coffee cake, it made me feel like I was getting away with something. I hope my kids are as confused as I was.

When I reread this recently, I couldn't help but to think of what would happen if coffee cake, typically left to cool before consumption, were served hot out of the pot? Just like a cup of coffee (cue the laugh track). Further, what if there was some element of the coffee cake that was totally unique to serve at high temperatures. Something to set the eating experience apart from all others. Then it dawned on me that the blueberry, when set to heat, essentially explodes. Blueberry lava makes up for the lamented lack of coffee in coffee cake.

—Howie

TOTAL TIME: 1 hour, 20 minutes | **VESSEL:** 3 qt Dutch oven | **SERVES:** 4–6

½ cup coconut milk
¾ cup granulated sugar
1 large egg
1 teaspoon vanilla extract
½ tsp kosher salt
Zest of 1 lime
½ cup extra-virgin olive oil, plus more for greasing
2⅔ cups all-purpose flour, divided
2 tsp baking powder
1 pint fresh blueberries
4 Tbsp butter, melted
⅓ cup brown sugar, packed

Preheat the oven to 350°F.

In a mixing bowl, whisk together coconut milk, sugar, egg, vanilla, salt, lime zest, and ½ cup of olive oil. In a separate mixing bowl, whisk together 2 cups of flour and baking powder. Stir the dry ingredients into the wet just until no dry flour is visible. Fold in the blueberries.

In a separate mixing bowl, combine melted butter with brown sugar. Add the remaining ⅔ cup of flour by hand until the mixture forms small crumbs that stick together when pinched. Set aside.

Grease a Dutch oven with olive oil. Pour the batter into the pot and smooth the top. Evenly top the batter with the brown sugar crumble. Gently press down to flatten the surface.

Transfer the pot to the oven and bake until the crumble on top is beginning to brown, about 50 to 60 minutes. Remove the coffee cake from the oven, let it rest for 10 minutes, then slice and serve piping hot!

100
200

It's My Jam

Well, maybe it's yours now

You're about to make the easiest jam and the easiest cookies of your life. At the same time. In one pot. This may be habit forming. Be careful out there.

—Greg

TOTAL TIME: 1 hour, 45 minutes | **VESSEL:** 3–4½ qt Dutch oven | **SERVES:** 4–6

½ cup granulated sugar
2 Tbsp water
18 oz mixed berries, lightly mashed
⅛ tsp kosher salt

Preheat the oven to 350°F.

Add sugar and water to a Dutch oven over medium-low heat. Stir as you check consistency. When the sugar has mostly dissolved, increase the heat to medium and continue to stir until the melted sugar has turned slightly darker. Turn off the heat and stir in berries and salt.

Cover with a lid and transfer to the oven for 15 minutes. This would be a great time to optionally butter the underside of the lid and add uncooked dough from Lid Cookies. Yes, *That* Lid Again from page 237.

Carefully remove the lid, and therefore the Lid Cookies. Continue to simmer the fruit for another 15 minutes. Remove the jam from the oven and allow to cool until it gels, about 1 hour.

Enjoy the jam with the accompanying cookies (if you're lucky enough to have made them), toast, English muffin, cornbread, or just a darned *spoon*, this stuff is so good.

Lid Cookies. Yes, *That* Lid Again

Love Nutella? Have two other ingredients?

TOTAL TIME: 20 minutes | **VESSEL:** Dutch oven lid | **SERVES:** 2–3

1 cup Nutella or other chocolate-nut spread
1 cup all-purpose flour
1 large egg

NOTE: This recipe presumes that you are already cooking another recipe from this book in the body of the Dutch oven that you will finish in the oven with the lid on for at least 15 minutes. It also presumes the oven temperature is set to 350°F.

In a stand mixer or a large mixing bowl by hand, combine all ingredients thoroughly. The texture may seem crumbly, but once you begin to work palmfuls into balls, they will take shape.

15 minutes before *It's My Jam* is set to be done cooking, place the Dutch oven lid securely upside down on a work surface and butter it. Grab some dough and make a small ball, flattening it into a puck shape. Repeat with remaining dough and carefully place the lid on top of the pot.

Transfer the otherwise filled Dutch oven with the lid on upside down to the oven and bake until the cookie just begin to set, about 12 to 15 minutes. Remove (at least) the pot lid from the oven and set the cookie aside until ready to eat!

Mission: Burn the Cheesecake

Basque in the glory of all things bittersweet

Last summer, my family and I took a break from the Barcelona tourist crowds and spent two weeks in San Sebastian in the Basque country of Spain. I was in my happy place. Two beaches from which to choose each day. Great surf. Perfectly warm August breezes. Dog-friendly town. Some of the best savory foods in Europe, nay, the world, just steps from our doorway. And, completely unexpectedly, the best darned cheesecake this side of Brooklyn.

The Basque cheesecake is at the same time familiar and a complete stranger. The usual sweetness is there, so the flavor profile of the inside is what you have come to love about cheesecake. But, the interior is so creamy, airy, and jiggly that you hurt yourself trying to figure out how it even stands up on its own. Wonder no more. The trick to this Continental cheesecake is the crust. Oh, it's not a separate crust. No graham crackers. No butter. No prebake. The crust is literally the same custard as the inside, but burnt into solidity.

Not only does this self-formed crust hold everything together but because of its unique overcookedness, it offers up a bittersweet experience like no other dessert. This cheesecake changes minds, and I believe our version stands up to those with whom I fell in love in San Sebastian.

—Howie

TOTAL TIME: 2 hours, 15 minutes | **VESSEL:** 4½+ qt Dutch oven | **SERVES:** 8–10

- 2 lb cream cheese, room temperature
- 1¼ cup granulated sugar
- 7 large eggs
- 2 cups heavy cream
- ½ cup all-purpose flour
- 1 tsp kosher salt
- 1 Tbsp canola or vegetable oil

Preheat the oven to 400°F.

In the bowl of a stand mixer fitted with a paddle, cream the cream cheese and sugar on medium speed until the sugar has dissolved, about 4 to 5 minutes. Add eggs one at time until they are all blended in. Scrape down the sides of the bowl as needed to ensure an even, consistent mixture. Add cream and allow it to fully incorporate. Sprinkle flour and salt across the top and continue to mix until the batter is extremely smooth, about 5 minutes.

Grease the insides of a Dutch oven with oil, then line with parchment paper, making sure to leave some overhang. It is wise to use two sheets of parchment in opposite directions to ensure that the batter will be fully encased as it bakes and rises. Pour the batter into the parchment paper–lined pot and transfer to the oven. Bake until the top is deep, dark brown, about 60 to 70 minutes.

Remove the cake from the oven and let it rest at room temperature for 1 hour. Carefully lift it out of the pot using the parchment paper as handles. Gently pull the parchment away from the sides of the cake. Slice warm, jiggly slices of utopian cheesecake goodness.

We Don't Need No Stinkin' Pine

Apple upside-down cake

Pineapple was my favorite fruit. I remember my one childhood trip to Hawaii, and the absolute joy being surrounded by pineapples. Pineapples on the beach. Pineapples in my drinks. And, best of all was a trip to the Dole pineapple cannery. I know, it's weird to be nine years old and to love a cannery. But all that pineapple! And, at the end, all you could eat and drink!

And then, one horrible night, after devouring my first pineapple of the season, I discovered a sad fact. I had become allergic to pineapple. No hives, no rashes, just stomach pain that made me long for a nice case of salmonella.

So here we are, ten years without pineapple. And I've survived. Some might even say thrived. If nothing else, my lack of pineapple allowed me to think of this amazing, moist, over-the-top apple-cinnamony cake.

Credit to the geniuses at *Cooks Illustrated* who thought of boiling dried apples in cider. For a bunch of cake bakers, they are some real smart cookies.

—Greg

TOTAL TIME: 1 hours, 30 minutes | **VESSEL:** 3 qt Dutch oven | **SERVES:** 8–10

- 1 cup apple cider
- 1 cup dried apple rings
- 1½ cups all-purpose flour
- 1 tsp baking soda
- 1 egg
- 1 cup unsweetened applesauce
- ¼ cup granulated sugar
- 1 tsp cinnamon or apple pie spice
- ½ tsp kosher salt
- ½ cup (1 stick) butter, melted, divided
- Powdered sugar to dust

Preheat the oven to 350°F.

Add cider and dried apples to a Dutch oven over low heat. Bring to barely bubbling and cook for 15 minutes. Remove the reconstituted apples but keep the reduced cider. Reserve 6 or more of the prettiest-looking apple rings. Chop up the remaining apples finely and set aside. Wipe out the Dutch oven.

In a mixing bowl, whisk together flour and baking soda.

In a separate mixing bowl, whisk together egg, applesauce, sugar, cinnamon or apple pie spice, salt, reduced cider, and 7 tablespoons of melted butter.

Mix the wet ingredients into the dry ingredients until no white flour is visible. Stir in the finely chopped apples.

Use the remaining 1 tablespoon of butter to coat the bottom and sides of the Dutch oven. Arrange the reserved prettiest rings of apple along the bottom of the pot. Gently pour the batter over the apple rings, trying to leave them in place on the bottom of the pot.

Place the pot in the oven and bake, uncovered, for 35 to 40 minutes, or until a toothpick inserted in the middle comes out clean.

Run a knife along the circumference of the cake to help it release. Place a platter on top of the Dutch oven and carefully turn it all over. Garnish with a dash of powdered sugar, slice, and enjoy!

That Baby Ain't Dutch

Seriously

This book may have been better titled, "Fun with Confusing Food Names!?" The "Dutch baby" pancake is not Dutch at all. I kind of wish it were Dutch. Then we would have a whopping *two* Dutch recipes in our Dutch oven cookbook! This puffy pancake recipe was originally *Deutsch*, or "German" in German! Structurally, the pancake is close to a huge popover, which of course is an American derivative of English Yorkshire pudding, minus the beef drippings. Recipes enjoy a proud provenance and they matter. Here's where it really burns my beard . . .

There actually exists a Dutch pancake that is small in stature, *poffertjes*. They're made in a specialized cast-iron pan with concave divots. Their also crafted with yeast, which makes it closer to a bread in the end. As the batter cooks along the domed bottom, a deft hand slowly turns the cake so that as it puffs to a perfect, light, crispy sphere. *This* is a true Dutch baby and I wish we could have a redo. Hey 1942, can we have our Dutch baby back? While we await their response, please enjoy our Dutch baby that ain't.

—Greg

TOTAL TIME: 30 minutes | **VESSEL:** 3+ qt Dutch oven | **SERVES:** 1–2

3 eggs
½ cup milk or nut milk
½ cup all-purpose flour
1 Tbsp granulated sugar
½ tsp vanilla extract
½ tsp kosher salt
¼ tsp cinnamon
5 Tbsp butter
Mixed berries for serving
Maple syrup for serving

Preheat the oven to 425°F with a Dutch oven inside.

In a blender, puree eggs, milk, flour, sugar, vanilla, salt, and cinnamon.

Carefully remove the heated pot from the oven, add butter, and swirl until it melts and begins to froth. Pour in batter and return the pot to the oven to bake until the edges have puffed and browned, about 18 to 20 minutes.

Serve hot with fresh berries and maple syrup.

Nutty Banana Goes Coconuts

One good fruit gone bad

There's always money in the banana stand. Why? Because frozen bananas—invented and still available on Balboa Island, California—are a delicious treat on a hot summer day.

But what to do on a Wednesday evening when you are far from the beach? Why, I've got the perfect idea. Roast some bananas in the old Dutch oven. Combined with chocolate, nuts, and a touch of coconut—you simply won't believe how good they are.

—Greg

TOTAL TIME: 20 min | **VESSEL:** 6 qt Dutch oven | **SERVES:** 4–6

6 ripe bananas, peeled
1 tsp vegetable or canola oil
¼ cup chopped pecans
2 Tbsp shredded coconut
¼ cup hot fudge, warmed

Preheat the oven to 425°F.

Place the bananas in the Dutch oven, and then pour in the oil. Toss to lightly coat all the bananas. Cover and place in the oven for 15 minutes.

Remove the Dutch oven from the oven. Sprinkle the bananas with the pecans and shredded coconut. Place back in the oven, uncovered, for 5 minutes.

Allow to cool for 5 minutes and serve with hot fudge.

About the Authors

Greg Matza and Howie Southworth are the best-selling authors of *One Pan to Rule them All: 100 Cast-Iron Skillet Recipes for Indoors and Out*, *Kiss my Casserole: 100 Mouthwatering Recipes Inspired by Ovens Around the World*, and *Chinese Street Food: Small Bites, Classic Recipes, and Harrowing Tales Across the Middle Kingdom*.

They first formed their creative partnership more than 25 years ago. This dynamic duo first met during college, working at a summer camp on the University of California campus in Santa Barbara. Be jealous. They became fast friends over Sammy Davis Jr. tunes, Freebirds burritos, and cans of Cactus Cooler.

Their early collaborations included amateur theater productions, ill-fated double dates, harrowing road trips, web series production, and epic dinner parties. These soirees were the seed of their culinary partnership, and continue to this day. Weeks are spent devising and preparing themed parties, which have ranged from A Pirate Feast to a 20-Course Chinese Banquet. Their dress code simply reads, "elastic."

When not near their stoves, Howie and Greg can likely be found eating their way across China. For this insatiable pair, going out for some Sichuan usually involves a trans-Pacific flight. Want to share in their culinary adventures? Visit them on @HowieAndGreg.

Conversion Charts

Metric and Imperial Conversions

(These conversions are rounded for convenience)

Ingredient	Cups/Tablespoons/ Teaspoons	Ounces	Grams/Milliliters
Butter	1 cup/ 16 tablespoons/ 2 sticks	8 ounces	230 grams
Cheese, shredded	1 cup	4 ounces	110 grams
Cream cheese	1 tablespoon	0.5 ounce	14.5 grams
Cornstarch	1 tablespoon	0.3 ounce	8 grams
Flour, all-purpose	1 cup/1 tablespoon	4.5 ounces/0.3 ounce	125 grams/8 grams
Flour, whole wheat	1 cup	4 ounces	120 grams
Fruit, dried	1 cup	4 ounces	120 grams
Fruits or veggies, chopped	1 cup	5 to 7 ounces	145 to 200 grams
Fruits or veggies, pureed	1 cup	8.5 ounces	245 grams
Honey, maple syrup, or corn syrup	1 tablespoon	0.75 ounce	20 grams
Liquids: cream, milk, water, or juice	1 cup	8 fluid ounces	240 milliliters
Oats	1 cup	5.5 ounces	150 grams
Salt	1 teaspoon	0.2 ounce	6 grams
Spices: cinnamon, cloves, ginger, or nutmeg (ground)	1 teaspoon	0.2 ounce	5 milliliters
Sugar, brown, firmly packed	1 cup	7 ounces	200 grams
Sugar, white	1 cup/1 tablespoon	7 ounces/0.5 ounce	200 grams/12.5 grams
Vanilla extract	1 teaspoon	0.2 ounce	4 grams

Oven Temperatures

Fahrenheit	Celsius	Gas Mark
225°	110°	1/4
250°	120°	1/2
275°	140°	1
300°	150°	2
325°	160°	3
350°	180°	4
375°	190°	5
400°	200°	6
425°	220°	7
450°	230°	8

Index

D

E

F

G